STONEHILL COLLEGE

"Securing the Vision"
*The Campaign for
Stonehill's Future*

Health Care Handbook

Health Care Handbook

A CONSUMER'S GUIDE

TO THE AMERICAN

HEALTH CARE SYSTEM

Mark Cromer

SANTA
MONICA
PRESS

Published by:
SANTA MONICA PRESS
P.O. Box 1076
Santa Monica, CA 90406-1076

Printed in the United States

This book is intended to provide general information. It is not intended to replace the advice of your physician or medical counselor. The publisher, author, distributor, and copyright owner are not engaged in rendering health, medical or other professional advice or services, and are not liable or responsible to any person or group with respect to any loss, illness or injury caused or alleged to be caused by the information found in this book.

Library of Congress Cataloging-in-Publication Data

Cromer, Mark, 1965—
Health care handbook : a consumer's guide to the American health care system / by Mark Cromer.
      p.   cm.
ISBN 0-9639946-7-0 (pbk.)
1. Hospital care.   2. Medical care.   3. Consumer education.
I. Title.
RA965.6.C76   1997
362.1 ' 0973—dc21   97-15262
                                                       CIP

10 9 8 7 6 5 4 3 2 1

Book and cover design by Mauna Eichner
Cartoons by Jorge Pacheco
Stethoscope image © 1997 PhotoDisc, Inc.

Contents

Acknowledgments

I didn't really write this book.

While I am a writer by both passion and trade (in that order), for this project I operated as part-journalist, part-distiller. Though I have worked in the health care industry for the past three years (as a media liaison for a rehabilitation hospital), I am certainly no expert in the field. Which is a good thing, perhaps. Experts tend to talk (and write) like experts and focus on things that experts need or want to know. Which is fine... for experts. But I wanted to write a book for the other 99.9% of us.

Of course, without experts I could never have compiled this guide.

I talked with a lot of people while researching the various chapters. I listened, took notes and attempted to distill, in the simplest of terms, the information they passed along. I felt like the lawyer Denzel Washington played in the film

Philadelphia, constantly asking these experts to "explain it to me like I was a three-year-old."

And they were gracious enough to do just that.

So I'd like to thank all of them for bearing with me, for taking my numerous phone calls and weathering my constant reminders of "Keep in mind this is a consumer's guide, don't get too technical on me!"

At Pomona Valley Hospital Medical Center, social worker Meagan Kramer was wonderful, helping me on this guide as well as on a couple of stories for the *Los Angeles Times*. Also at Pomona Valley was Dr. Brian Tiep, the pulmonary specialist who is simply one of the best friends anyone's lungs could have (Phillip Morris beware).

Over on the other side of Kellogg Hill there is the Citrus Valley Medical Center, a group of hospitals that includes Queen of the Valley in West Covina and Inter-Community in Covina. Catherine Koetters in the Public Relations Department was a terrific help, taking my repeated requests for sources. Requests that usually went something like, "I need a maternity specialist in about 15 minutes. Can you set me up?" Catherine introduced me to professionals like Chelly Coon, Director of Maternity and Child Health; Jill McCormick, Assistant Director of Oncology; Pam Karns, Program Director of Cardiovascular and Critical Care Services; and Cathy Kaliel, Director of Emergency Services.

At Loma Linda University Children's Hospital in Loma Linda, I was assisted by Dr. Ron Perkin, Director of the Pediatric Intensive Care Unit, and Katy Dalke, Nurse Manager of the hospital's PICU.

George Pappas at Miller, Geer & Associates was kind

Acknowledgments

enough to steer me to John Calderone, President and CEO of Corona Medical Center, whose insights on the evolution of the health care system can be found in the foreword.

Kathy Wolf, an RN in Cambridge who has studied the evolution of nursing in the United States, was gracious enough to take a late-night interview with me.

At Casa Colina Centers for Rehabilitation in Pomona there are many people I'd like to thank, starting with the entire staff, but narrowed down a bit to Fred Aronow (for not firing me outright as I worked on this project, as well as for his proofing help), John Freeland, Michele Betts, Rosie Fernandez, Wendy Carns, Ross Lesins, Michelle Stoddard (for the laughs and booze), Andy Houghton and David Kiley (for making wheelchair sports look cool, which is more important than you know), Anne Johnson (for doing Lewis and Clark proud by forging new frontiers with Outdoor Adventures) and Dale Eazell (for pushing Casa Colina repeatedly into the future, which is where it needs to be).

I'd also like to thank Dr. George Ulett, Robert Davis, Gerald Stockman and my uncle Walt Weis, who was nice enough to fly back from Baja to help me with this project.

My deep appreciation to Raechel Fittante, who didn't laugh me out of the room when I asked if she'd be my assistant.

To Jeffrey Goldman, for seeing the need for this guide and acting on it.

And to Antrese, for never revoking my snuggle privileges even when I was working on this guide until the wee hours of the morning. I couldn't have done it without her, not to mention all those other things.

MARK CROMER

Foreword

BY JOHN A. CALDERONE, PH.D.

Although the art and science of medicine in the U.S. is sometimes shrouded behind the surgeon's mask, there is no question about the fact that our care is considered the best in the world. The foundation for this high quality of care is based on a concept that is basically simple: diagnosis and treatment are determined by a patient's highly-trained physician and paid for by the government, a private insurance plan or the patient himself.

Yet today's changing concept of health care is hardly so simple. Most of us believe that if we are not sick, then we are healthy, or that the absence of illness is good health. In that sense, the term "health care" can then be seen as an effort by medical professionals to treat and cure sickness.

But it is also apparent that even the best medical care, purchased with the most expensive health plan, cannot cure all illness. Furthermore, today's medical care is not always sufficient to help patients regain their health. I am convinced that to fully enhance your lifestyle, you need to take a more proactive role in your own health care. That means understanding your own and your family's health care needs, committing to wellness and making lifestyle choices about what you eat, drink and how active you are, among other decisions.

From my vantage point as a hospital administrator, each day I see people treated for diseases that could have been prevented. I see their families wait anxiously in the lobby for their doctor to tell them the bad or good news about a loved one. On top of this, the family is probably concerned about who is going to pay for all the care, or what may or may not be covered under their new "managed care plan."

The rapid and sometimes bewildering pace of change in health care today, fueled by the rise of "managed care," has increasingly forced consumers and those that provide care to face tough issues.

How can patients access low-cost, high-quality health care? Why can't I see my own doctor? How long do I have to wait to see my doctor?

The answers are hardly simple.

Employers and insurance companies are bringing tremendous pressure to bear on hospitals and physicians to reduce costs. Advanced technology and new medications are expensive. As patients, we may demand the very best, but are we willing to pay more out of our own pocket for it? That question still remains unanswered, but it underscores the point of finding a balance between cost and benefit.

To hold down costs, the response from hospitals and

doctors has been a health care revolution in which there have been several main advances under the auspices of "managed care"—consolidation of services, restriction to expensive specialty care and reduced health care costs.

Among other noticeable elements, this revolution has heated up competition among health care providers. Marketing and advertising efforts have been intensified. But which hospital do you go to? A large medical center or a smaller community hospital? If both hospitals serve the community, is there a difference in care? Is there a difference in cost?

Like consumers, physicians themselves are also playing an increasingly important role in the change of health care. In the last few years, chances are good that your physician is no longer in private practice as we have come to know it. Your doctor has probably joined with another group of doctors to form a network that allows the physicians to contract with a variety of health plans.

With little out-of-pocket expenses to the patient, managed care plans have become very popular. The ultimate goal of managed care is to create organizations that can bring together doctors and hospitals to reduce costs, while at the same time increasing quality and access to the system for patients. Important success factors in these health care networks include more emphasis on measuring clinical effectiveness (what works and what doesn't for specific diseases), achieving greater cost-effectiveness through better quality ("let's do it right the first time"), re-engineering of patient care (sicker patients get more care, those less ill go home more quickly) and streamlining management (more nurses, less supervisors).

But what does that mean for you, the consumer of health care? The good news is that for health care, this is the "age of the consumer." What patients really want (like all of us) is quality care and help navigating these sometimes rough waters.

In the final analysis, that means these new concepts in managed care create a seamless system for patients who need physicians and access to a variety of services such as emergency care, rehabilitation, outpatient surgery, home health care, skilled nursing care and more. The range of alternatives is intended to promote patient care in the most appropriate, least restrictive setting.

With these changes in health care, more and more patients are discovering that it is in their best interest to take a greater responsibility for their own well-being. Patients are becoming more involved in their own care from self-screening to being knowledgeable about treatment options *before* they visit their doctor.

That's where health education comes in. Good information about your health care options is essential to help reduce demand for health care services by allowing consumers to take more responsibility for managing their own care. This is one of the main reasons that hospitals offer community education programs and classes. It makes sense for everyone involved.

Through technology, increased access to health care information is also having a major impact for millions of Americans. The abundance of health care information available on the internet is changing the relationship between patients, physicians and hospitals. Although it should not serve as a substitute for professional medical services, there is a clear benefit to easy access to medical information. Not only does it cut costs and save both patients and doctors time, but also allows individuals seeking medical advice to remain anonymous and conduct research in the privacy of their own home. The ease of obtaining information from one's home can be particularly relevant for homebound elderly and disabled persons. From a psychological point of view, the internet breaks barriers of distance to dissolve the feeling of loneliness and isolation brought on by debilitating diseases. Easily accessible information and support via the internet can and does empower patients and their families.

Despite the proliferation of health care information available to consumers, it's still difficult to know how to choose a physician, a health plan or a hospital. But information can help consumers sensibly make choices that suit their needs.

In considering a fee-for-service system, managed care organization or any other payer system, there are no objective means of separating good physicians from less capable ones. All types of health care organizations have a variety of mechanisms in place that supposedly are designed to eliminate poor sources of health care and to identify good sources. Consumer knowledge and education are key.

In this age of consumerism, we see a very intense effort to rank health care organizations, such as the *U.S. News and World Report* on hospitals, colleges and the like. Regional magazines often have an issue featuring who are the best doctors in their area. How do they know? They really don't, beyond the opinion of other doctors. These publications still remain, however, a good source—or at the very least, a place to start.

Once informed, people are surprised to learn how much uncertainty there is in medical care and how many trade-offs exist. Today, people have more insight into what medical professionals do, why they do it and the chances of success or failure involved.

Reforms initiated by the health care industry are bringing down costs, and it's going to continue. Health care spending is down. Government-sponsored health reforms would further control costs through cuts in the rate of growth of Medicare and Medicaid spending, which combined with the increase in demand will cause real cuts in health care costs. The budget cuts and heavy discounts are putting a financial strain on hospitals and physicians. If they are to survive, they must continue to make aggressive cost reductions while increasing quality. And studies have found that as quality goes up costs go down. In that case, everybody wins.

Our biggest challenge in reshaping health care for the future is the challenge of leadership. Today's effective leader is an agent of change. One lesson kids learn from playing video games is that standing still will get them "zapped" quicker than anything else. We in health care have learned the same lessons.

It is clear that today's health care is an interactive process involving various entities, but ultimately health care is in the control of the individual. Self-empowerment leads to positive changes—in your health, the care you receive and, quite remarkably, public policy.

Foreword

By reading the *Health Care Handbook*, you will have made the first step toward understanding the complex world of health care. The more you learn, the better chance you have of maintaining good health. So if you or your loved ones should need the services of a health care provider, the more you know, the better your care will prove efficient and effective.

John A. Calderone, Ph.D., is a veteran health care executive with more than 25 years of experience in both clinical and administrative positions. He currently serves as chief executive officer of Corona Regional Medical Center, an acute care facility in Corona, California.

Introduction

It started with a mild sore throat and climaxed with a week-long stay in a major medical center. By the time it was over, my baptism into the health care system had been a twisting roller coaster ride that taught me two important lessons: 1) I knew relatively nothing about the vast, jumbled system that provides for our health care and 2) Had I been a little more educated and interested in my own health care, I could have saved myself a lot of misery and money. Like most Americans, I knew more about my car and auto repair shops than I did about my body and our nation's health care system.

It was the summer of 1986 and I had just returned from an extensive road trip through western Canada. I arrived back home in Southern California just in time to start my first quarter at Cal Poly Pomona.

All through that first week of school my throat was bothering me, getting progressively worse despite the steady stream of lozenges and herbal teas with which I was treating it. I also found myself tired all the time, and was falling asleep by 7:00 p.m. I knew the first week at a university was going to be hectic, but this was ridiculous. I suspected something was dramatically wrong by the second week of school when I could barely keep my eyes open in class and my throat hurt so bad that I tried to hold off swallowing for as long as possible.

I finally trudged into the university's Health Center, worried I had waited a little too long before seeking treatment, yet reassured that I would now get it taken care of quickly. I chose to go to my school's clinic first, as it was more convenient and I wanted to save my parents the deductible a visit to our family doctor would have cost them. I never would have imagined, as I walked into the Health Center that day, that only a week later I would be sprawled across a hospital bed at a major regional medical center, IVs running into my body and my throat nearly swollen shut.

At the university clinic that day, I filled out my forms (proving I was a student and thus qualifying for care that students pay for through their admissions fees) and waited to be seen. A nurse-practitioner was the first one to evaluate me. "You probably have mono," she said.

"The kissing disease?" I asked, wondering about a girl in Vancouver I had necked with just a few weeks before.

"Well, you can get it a lot of ways," she said. "But it really knocks you for a loop."

The doctor came into the room and checked me out. The nurse asked him if he wanted to order a "mono scan."

He looked down at his clipboard for a moment and then said "No, put him on tetracycline and Sudafed." He looked back at me. "If you don't feel any better in a week or so, come back and see us." Famous last words.

I remember that the nurse seemed puzzled by the doctor's decision not to order a mono scan, but she didn't say anything and I didn't either. After all, I had been checked out and was getting some drugs that were supposed to do the job. I was in good hands.

Two days later, my condition had worsened enough that my mother drove me to our family doctor, who seemed concerned that my tonsils (which I could never see before) were now on prominent display in the back of my throat. Again, mononucleosis came up, but no blood was drawn for a scan. Instead, he sent me over to an ear, nose and throat specialist, who checked to see if I might have an abscess in the back of my throat.

The specialist determined I didn't have an abscess, but gave me a big shot of antibiotics and a large brown bottle full of liquid codeine. He told me I should start feeling better in a couple of days—"once the antibiotics start taking hold"—and said I should call my primary care doctor if I wasn't getting better by the following week.

The next morning, I woke up to find my tonsils were big enough to conceal the back of my throat and had turned a nice shade of white. It hurt too much to swallow the codeine and my vision was starting to get blurry. I felt nauseous.

I called my doctor's office and told them I was getting worse.

The receptionist asked if I wanted to make an appointment for the next day. I told her I'd be dead by then. She put me on hold for a moment and then the doctor got on the line. I explained my condition and he told me to meet him at the hospital. My parents were at work so a friend drove me to the emergency room.

My doctor ordered a battery of tests and lo and behold, if it wasn't our old friend mononucleosis after all! By this time the mono had had an uncontested field day in my body for several weeks. My throat was so swollen I could not eat or drink (I was dehydrating prior to being admitted in the hospital) and just keeping my eyes open for more than a couple of hours at a time was a struggle.

I spent about a week in the hospital, where I was kept on IVs. By the time I checked out I had dropped more than 10 pounds off an already thin frame. I spent two more weeks at home, staying in bed for 18 to 20 hour stretches. When I finally returned to school, I had missed nearly half the quarter.

The lessons of my brush with mono were many, some of them quite costly to my body, my parent's insurance company and my academic standing that first quarter at the university. But they were valuable lessons as well.

If I were to go through that same situation now, more than a decade later, I know I would approach it in a much different manner, which in turn might have affected how sick I became and how much money and time I spent on my treatment.

I would have certainly questioned the doctor at the Health Center that day about why he didn't want to run a mono scan right then, especially after the nurse-practitioner seemed to think I had mono (based on my symptoms) and suggested the scan to the doctor. I would have asked him if he didn't think I had mono, then what was it he thought I might have. Looking back, I can't remember that he actually gave me a specific diagnosis at all.

Today I would ask him how effectively he thought the tetracycline and Sudafed were going to be and how quickly they would act. Were there other drugs or treatment options? I also would have asked him what the risks were in delaying a test for mono. Depending on what he told me, I would have asked for a mono test there or, more likely, would have driven over to my family doctor and sought a diagnosis from him.

In short, if I were to go through it all again today, I would have been a much more actively involved participant in my heath care, asking more questions much sooner and expecting fair answers.

My miserable brush with mononucleosis was the first big step in my evolution as a health care consumer. It was the wake-up call I needed. As a result of my sickness I realized that in times of serious injury or illness, my health would depend on a system I knew next to nothing about. This was highlighted when I was admitted to the hospital that day. I remember sitting in a wheelchair in the emergency room, signing forms which I hadn't read and asking my friend to call my mother to get her insurance policy numbers (evidently never thinking I may need to have those on me at any given time).

I had no idea what to expect of my stay in the hospital, besides the nagging notion that if my throat ever recovered to the point where I could eat, the food probably wouldn't taste too good ("One step above prison grub and one below airline food," a friend remarked. "Save your appetite for when you get home." This eventually proved to be untrue.) What should I have my mother bring me? A suitcase full of clothes? Books and magazines? A radio? Could I really use any of this stuff? Was it allowed? Was I confusing a hospital with a hotel?

And who was going to take care of me? Nurses? What about bathing and using the bathroom? While they didn't pertain to my immediate medical status, these questions and others really mattered to me. The unknown can be unnerving and unsettling, to say the least.

The next big step I took in becoming a better health care consumer occurred about eight years later, when I left my job as a daily newspaper reporter and went to work at Casa Colina Centers for Rehabilitation, one of the top medical rehabilitation institutions in the nation. I joined the non-profit rehab center's public relations department as a media liaison, which meant I would be working with reporters who were covering stories on people who were recovering from traumatic illnesses and injuries. Casa Colina works with many "high profile" patients, so there's always a reporter, photographer or a camera crew around.

My tenure at Casa Colina has raised my consciousness about health care several levels, completely reinforcing my belief that as consumers we not only have rights but, perhaps more importantly, we have *responsibilities*. And that the more we fulfill our responsibilities as patients, the more likely we will be able to understand and enjoy our rights as health care consumers.

But working at Casa Colina also showed me that a lot of people still go through the motions when it comes to their health care. I saw (and continue to see) patients who ask few if any questions of their doctor or therapist, though one can tell by the look on their faces they have a thousand questions floating around in their heads. I'm always amazed to see someone who has suffered a life-altering traumatic injury, like a gunshot wound that has severed the spinal cord, sit silently as the therapist explains things to them. I imagine I would be asking so many questions they'd have to drag me out of my session.

While watching these uninformed patients has been depressing, I've also been inspired by those people with disabilities who are determined to take control of their lives. They start by becoming active participants in their health care. Most of them would probably admit that they did so because health care has taken on a more central role in their daily lives, and they understand they can no longer afford to be disconnected and uneducated. But while the stakes may be slightly higher in the immediate sense for them, it's clear that we all could benefit immensely from just knowing a little more than we already do about our health care system. Indeed, there are few places where the old adage of "Knowledge is Power" is more true than in the world of health care.

It is my hope that *Health Care Handbook* will give you the knowledge and the power to obtain the best health care the American system has to offer.

Enjoy.

Health Plans: The Choice is Yours

"When the praying does no good,
insurance does help."

BERTOLT BRECHT

 If you become seriously ill or injured, the cost of your health care can be astronomical. You've probably heard of those cases where families not covered by health insurance have sold their homes and possessions just to pay for the cost of treating a loved one suffering from a disease. While this is an extreme situation, it highlights the fact that going through life without health insurance is like swimming on a beach with signs posted which read "Warning: Shark-infested Waters!" In short, you're taking a big chance.

Yet just like the health care system itself, health insurance is a big and complicated world, one which most people know little to nothing about. As a consumer, you don't need to be an expert in health insurance, but you should have a basic understanding of how coverage works and what sort of health plan would best meet your needs.

When most people get insurance, usually through an employer-offered plan, they immediately feel secure. "Hey, I'm covered!" they tell themselves. Maybe they are, and maybe they aren't. Unfortunately, it's usually after an accident or illness when they find out that some important element of their treatment is either not covered or significantly limited by their health insurance policy. By then, in many instances, it's too late.

Rosie Fernandez, a Certified Case Manager for Casa Colina Hospital, has worked as a liaison between the hospital, patient and insurance companies for the past 11 years. While specializing in rehabilitation, Fernandez says she has seen many people get a rude awakening when they are injured and are forced to pore over their policy—or have it explained to them—for the first time.

"The bottom line is this: *Read* your plan's handbook. Twice. Dig in," she says. "Most people get it, toss it in a filing cabinet and then try to remember where it is when they need it."

SHOPPING FOR INSURANCE

When you are preparing to buy a health plan, either through your employer (who usually offers several plans from which to choose) or on your own, there are several standard types of insurance to consider, from managed care plans to traditional fee-for-service indemnity plans. Explore your options carefully! Once enrolled in a plan at work it is usually not easy to switch until the next enrollment period, which typically comes every six months to a year.

What to Look for

Location If the health plan you are considering restricts or limits who can treat you, determine where these doctors and hospitals are located and think about convenience. Also find out how busy these doctors and hospitals are. For instance, how long will you typically have to wait to get an appointment with a particular doctor?

Quality Once you have the general feel for the doctors and hospitals in the health plan, seek out various credentials. For example, have any of the hospitals in the group been ranked in the Top 100 Hospitals by the HCIA-Mercer group? (See Appendix D.) What sort of references do the doctors who will potentially be treating you have? Ask for referrals to patients of both the doctors and the hospitals.

Cost Obvious, but important enough to stress. What are your co-payments for doctor office visits, emergency room visits, preventative care and prescription drugs?

Choice If you are considering a managed care plan, determine the scope of choice you'll have with doctors, hospitals and specialists. Are you limited to just a few doctors and hospitals, or are there dozens from which you can choose?

HMOS AND OTHER HEALTH PLANS

The following are basic definitions for some of the types of plans you'll be encountering when reading about your options:

HMO

This stands for Health Maintenance Organization. These are health plans that contract with physician groups and hospitals to provide comprehensive care to its members. Working under a system known as "capitation," the HMO pays these doctors and hospitals a set amount every month, regardless of how many patients from the HMO end up utilizing care. This approach has come under attack from some consumer advocates, who argue that what the industry considers to be an incentive to keep costs down (by reigning in unnecessary and expensive tests) is really leading to late diagnosis of ailments and postponement of treatments, as well as other problems. However, many members of HMOs are completely satisfied with the efficient and low-cost health care service an HMO can provide.

If you enroll in an HMO, you will be required to select a primary care doctor from the group of physicians participating in that HMO. Some HMOs own and operate their own hospitals and medical groups, while others contract services out. Non-emergency treatments beyond that doctor's scope of expertise are likely to be carried out by a specialist who is also within the HMO. Treatment by specialists outside of the HMO generally has to be approved beforehand.

An HMO will cover emergency care at hospitals and clinics outside of its contract group, but once you are stable enough to be transferred, it is likely you will be moved to a hospital under contract with your HMO. Emergency room visits for non-emergencies, as determined by the doctor on duty, may end up costing you money.

According to the American Managed Care and Review Association, there are five different types of HMOs:

IPA Independent Physician Association. An HMO will contract directly with an independent doctor or a group of doctors for services. These doctors have "solo" practices (thus the term "independent") and may treat a substantial number of non-HMO patients.

Group Model The HMO will contract services from a multi-specialty medical group or groups that may or may not work exclusively for the HMO.

Network Essentially a hybrid of the IPA and Group Model, the Network model is an HMO which contracts services from a variety of medical groups.

Staff Model Doctors and hospitals work exclusively for the HMO and treat only patients from that HMO. Kaiser Permanente pioneered the HMO concept with this model.

POS Point-of-Service plan. This type of HMO sometimes appears as an option in other plans and gives the consumer the choice of receiving treatment outside the HMO's standard network of care providers, albeit at a higher cost to the consumer.

PPO

This is a Preferred Provider Organization, which is a type of managed care. PPOs are unions of physicians, hospitals, employers, insurance companies and patient groups in which payment for services has been pre-negotiated. If you are in a PPO, you will have an incentive to use a doctor or hospital in the PPO, in the form of a lower co-payment and less paperwork (or no paperwork). One advantage to a PPO (depending on what your needs are) is that you can use a physician not in the PPO and still be covered, but at a non-discounted rate (i.e., your co-payment may be $30 instead of $5).

EPO

This is an Exclusive Provider Organization, which is essentially a hybrid of a PPO and an HMO, in which employers agree not to offer plans from any other insurance carrier. If you are in an EPO, you cannot go out of the system unless you want to spend your own money.

Fee-for-Service

These are the traditional types of insurance plans, which generally allow you greater flexibility in choosing doctors and hospitals. For example, a standard fee-for-service plan may pay 80% of your medical costs up to $5,000 and then 100% of the costs after that, BUT, you may have an annual deductible of $250 which must be reached before any coverage kicks in. A relatively healthy person who only goes to the doctor once or twice a year is likely to pay just under his deductible each year. An HMO or PPO, by contrast, usually requires a small co-payment (around $5) at each doctor's visit. The premiums for a fee-for-service plan may be slightly higher than managed care plans.

Limits, Coverages and Other Details

Because of the radically competitive market, many health plans are offering consumer-oriented perks to those who enroll in their plan. Such perks vary and may be geared to families (with an emphasis on maternity care) or seniors, but Fernandez says while these are nice touches, they should not deter you from getting down to the brass tacks of what your policy really gives you in the event of a traumatic injury or illness.

Here are a few questions to ask and some things to remember when shopping for a health plan:

Plan Limits Different plans will have different dollar caps or plan maximums (the amount spent when you've used all of your coverage up), usually ranging from one to five million dollars. Don't let the high figure fool you: if you became seriously sick or injured and require years of care in and out of hospitals, that million bucks will go a lot faster than you might imagine. So limits are important. HMOs often don't have dollar caps, which can be an advantage.

Catastrophic Coverage Double check any prospective plan for catastrophic coverage, and determine its limits and restrictions. Most people get insurance while only considering emergency care and standard hospital care coverage, but it usually takes more than that to get well and someone has to pay for it. Catastrophic coverage extends your treatment beyond the general acute care hospital, allowing you to receive medical rehabilitation, such as physical, occupational and speech therapy. Ask if there is a day limitation to the coverage, as plans will often restrict rehabilitation under catastrophic coverage to 30 days or 45 days. Determine whether these days are going to be inpatient or outpatient. This is very important. Patients have been wheeled out of their

Health Plans: The choice is yours.

rehab hospital room after a week or two, once their limit has been hit, and sent home to pursue their rehabilitation on an outpatient basis. Seek catastrophic coverage that does not set a limited number of days. Also, find out where rehabilitation is expected to take place. Some plans may stipulate that you have to receive it in a skilled nursing facility, which may not be as specialized or as focused on rehab as a hospital that specializes in rehabilitation.

Home Health Look for a plan that covers home health care benefits, as this type of care is becoming increasingly more important as hospital stays become shorter. Does your policy include a skilled nursing provision? Keep in mind that home health care extends far beyond a nurse swinging by your house once a day to check your temperature and look you over. Home care can include a range of rehabilitative therapies (physical, occupational and speech), IV administration, nutrition counseling and other types of care as well as social services. Find out what limitations your plan may place on this service.

Exclusions Your plan may specifically exclude coverage for certain illnesses or treatments. For example, many older insurance plans—many of which are still in effect—exclude occupational therapy from coverage. You should ask if there are any exclusions and exactly what they entail.

Diagnostic Related Groups Some health plans may limit care based on diagnostic related groups (DRGs), which basically means that the time you will spend in a hospital will depend on what you are getting treated for, NOT necessarily how well you are doing or how fast you are recovering. For example, a woman being hospitalized to undergo a radical mastectomy may be sent home within 24 hours if her health plan's DRG calls for discharge at that time. A treating physician can appeal that discharge time, but usually has to demonstrate that the patient is medically unstable and should not be released. Find out if a health care plan you are considering uses DRGs and, if so, in what instances. Take a look at them and make sure you feel comfortable with the time frames; also consult your doctor.

Appeals/Grievances Health plans have appeal systems built into them, processes for plan members to use in the event they have a complaint or want to challenge a decision (usually to deny coverage or length of stay). It's important that you find out what the exact appeal process is for any health care plan in which you are considering enrolling.

In most instances, your first line of appeal will be your doctor or the attending physician, who in turn will consult with the health plan. If you are not satisfied with the result, your next channel of appeal will probably be to the plan's medical director (who is an M.D.). But appeal procedures vary, so it's important to find out how the process works, who you need to contact and how to contact them at each step of the way.

Find out if the plan has an expedited or "emergency" appeals process and under what circumstances you can use such a process. What you might consider to be an emergency may not be officially recognized as one by the health plan. Again, the golden rule here is to find out before you enroll.

Medical Records If you ever find yourself filing a grievance or appealing a decision by your health plan, you will probably need to get of a copy of your medical records. Fortunately, there are laws in place that give patients the right to review and copy their records. If you request a copy of your medical file, you will be asked to sign a release form and will most likely be charged a small fee to cover the cost of copying the file. You may also grant access to your medical records to a third party, such as an attorney, but again you will have to sign a release allowing such access.

Note: Once you have exhausted the appeal process of your health plan, you might consider contacting the agency that regulates insurance companies in your state. In California, for example, the state's Department of Corporations regulates health plans and offers a toll-free number (1-800-400-0815) for consumers to report complaints. Be sure that you have gone through the entire appeal process before contacting the state agency. If you have an emergency grievance, you should contact the state agency directly. Check Appendix E for the number of the agency in your state.

LONG-TERM CARE

A long-term care plan covers you in the event you need extended custodial care, such as a skilled nursing facility (a "nursing home"). Considering the staggering cost of such care, it is surprising that only an estimated 8% of Americans currently have long-term care insurance coverage.

Robert Davis, president of Long-Term Care Quote, a company that researches long-term plans for consumers, says many people wait too long before investigating and buying a policy. "We get calls from people in their 90s," Davis says. "Their premiums are going to reflect that."

Davis says consumers should start considering different plans by the age of 50 and not wait much longer than that to buy one. "A lot of people think they'll wait until they're in their late 60s before they buy a plan and save all those premium payments," he says. "But they are taking a huge risk. They are gambling that their health will remain good and they won't need long-term care before then." Davis says people can be denied if their health is not good.

Prices are generally low for people in their 50s, with an average plan running about $800 per year. In comparison, an average plan for a person who is 68 (the age when most people start purchasing long-term care) costs about $1,500 per year. "The bottom line," notes Davis, "is that a couple in their 50s can get a real Cadillac plan, with very good coverage, for a very reasonable price."

Long-term care premiums are not fixed and can rise, Davis says, though they generally remain level. Premiums cannot be raised on individuals, but must be increased statewide and only after the state's insurance commissioner approves the hike. One of the services Davis's company provides is a background check on whether or not a company has raised its rates, and the amount, if any, by which the premiums rose.

Davis adds that though there are probably more than 100 different long-term care policies available to consumers today, almost 90% of the market is controlled by just a dozen companies.

Features to Consider

When shopping for a long-term care policy, Davis advises consumers to consider the following four areas:

Standard Features The basic provisions of long-term plans tend to vary little from provider to provider. Still, it is always a good idea to read through them carefully.

Important Features These are elements such as benefit "triggers" (what has to happen before benefits kick in?) and reimbursement details (how and when will you get paid or your care be covered?).

Special Features These are options built into a plan that are offered free of charge.

Optional Features These are features, such as benefit period (how long you are covered, which can range from one year to a lifetime, depending on what you want to buy), that you can obtain for an additional fee. Davis notes the average American will spend two and one-half years in a skilled nursing facility, so a three year plan is a good baseline to start from when considering a plan.

Davis also advises consumers to seek an integrated policy—one that will cover home health care, assisted living centers and adult day health care as well as a traditional skilled nursing facility.

FREE CARE AND
CHARITY CARE

Almost every hospital in the country provides some degree of free care, though that doesn't mean they do it out of the kindness of their institutional hearts. While charity certainly figures into some of the free care that's given by hospitals every year, much of it also falls under the category of bad debt or uncollected hospital bills.

Charity care is planned for by most hospitals just like any other budget item. How often and how much charity care a particular hospital provides every year will depend upon a variety of factors, such as the financial condition of the hospital, its mission statement and the needs of the community it serves.

For the uninsured and underinsured, hospitals can and do provide charity care on a certain basis, but these cases are relatively few compared to their overall patient totals. Hospitals usually determine a charity care patient in advance of treatment. Sometimes this can occur during the admission process, and in certain instances they will actually *offer* their services to the patient.

To find out a hospital's standard policy on charity care, call the patient services department. There may also be charity groups in your area that work with hospitals and doctors to provide charity care to certain people in need.

In the case of a medical emergency, hospitals are required by law to treat you whether or not you can pay the bill. Once your condition has stabilized, however, you will more than likely be transferred to a county or government-operated facility for additional care if you don't have insurance or can't afford to pay.

In most cases, doctors and hospitals are willing to work with you to arrange a reasonable payment plan if you would like to be treated by them but don't have insurance or enough insurance. The key word here is "reasonable." Before you sign a financial responsibility form committing you to the payment of the bill, the hospital will probably want to do an employment and asset evaluation to make sure your signature on the contract actually means something. If you don't have a job or any assets, it's not likely that you'll get a payment plan option.

SENIORS AND KIDS

If you are a married couple either with children or expecting to have children, it's important that you investigate a health plan's access to pediatricians and whether or not they have a children's hospital in their network (or whether you'll have access to a children's hospital if needed). Get a list of their pediatricians (doctors who specialize in the treatment of children) and then research those doctors, getting references, etc.

By the same token, if you are a senior and heading into what should be the golden years of your life, you don't need additional hassles from your health plan. Accordingly, investigate whether or not you will have access to doctors who specialize—or have a lot of experience in—treating seniors and the elderly. The location of these doctors and associated services can take on additional importance for seniors, *so make sure they are close by and easily accessible!*

HOSPICE CARE

In short, a hospice is a place you go to die—with dignity. No bundle of tubes snaking into your body from life-support machines, no hopelessly impossible life-saving measures, and no last ditch "Hail Mary" medical procedures. A hospice provides a warm, home-like environment where the focus is on making you as comfortable as possible while awaiting the inevitable.

With the appearance of AIDS, hospice care in America has grown dramatically, though hospices care for people with an array of terminal illnesses.

Health plans can cover hospice care and you should check for that provision specifically. Ask your plan's representative if hospice care is provided, what the day or time limits are, if any, and ask him to specify any other limitations that may be attached to the care.

MEDICARE AND MEDICAID

Other sources of benefits you may be entitled to that can help cover the cost of your medical care are Medicare and Medicaid, both massive government programs established to assist senior citizens and the poor, respectively. If you qualify for these benefits, they can usually be applied to a variety of different kinds of care, from hospitalization to adult day health care to home care. Consult your local Medicare or Medicaid office to see if you qualify for assistance.

CHAPTER 2

The Family Doctor: Your Partner in Good Health

"To avoid delay, please have all
your symptoms ready."

**NOTICE IN AN ENGLISH DOCTOR'S
WAITING ROOM**

"By combining our strengths—excellence in clinical care education and delivery from the academic institutions and population-based data analysis and wellness management experience from managed care—we can improve the quality of health care while also delivering it efficiently so it can be widely afforded."

What?

I read that epic sentence about five times before I could

even come close to digesting what the author was trying to say. The language was pulled directly from a press release by a major HMO which had just funded a research grant. While the release was geared to academia and the media, its language and style are good examples of the problem confronting many consumers as they wind their way through the health care system, i.e., trying to make sense out of what medical professionals are trying to tell them.

The fact is that even today, with more people taking an active role in their health care, many doctors and other health professionals continue to use language that is loaded with "medicalise" (language used by health care pros), and that is simply too obscure or technical for the average consumer to comprehend. Most of us have experienced this at one time or another, and we're usually too afraid or embarrassed to admit to our doctors that we don't understand what they've just told us. It's almost as if we're embarrassed that we didn't graduate from med school too! So we just nod our heads, make affirmative grunting sounds as if we understand precisely what we're being told, pick up our prescription and walk out feeling frustrated and, in extreme instances, powerless over what is happening. If you are shopping around for a physician, it is extremely important to pay close attention to any prospective doctor's ability to communicate clearly and effectively.

CHOOSING A DOCTOR

Gerald Stockman, a former state senator from New Jersey and an attorney who specializes in medical malpractice, says if he were shopping for a new primary care physician, he would also consider several other factors beyond good communication skills.

Stockman believes consumers should consider the following when shopping for a doctor:

▸ Is he a successful doctor? What does his practice look like? Where is it located? It is often a good sign if the physician seems to be moving up in his trade.

▸ What's his academic background? "I'd like to have at least heard of the school where he graduated from," Stockman says. Also ask for a list of the associations to which he belongs.

▸ If the doctor's not American, focus on his communication skills even more than usual. "I want a doctor who will understand me and who will make me understand him," Stockman says. Besides language, foreign-trained physicians often face cultural hurdles in the U.S. as well.

▸ Is he too specialized? For a primary care doctor, Stockman says he would want an internal medicine physician. Internists generally have broad diagnostic backgrounds.

▸ Word-of-mouth from neighbors and friends is good, but professional referrals are better, Stockman says. Find out where the doctor has admitting privileges and talk with the hospital's nursing staff about him. Ask the doctor for patient referrals as well.

▸ As a rule of thumb, Stockman says the more professional and sophisticated a doctor is, the more open he tends to be. If he is uptight and defensive, it could mean he lacks confidence, and that can be dangerous.

TALKING WITH YOUR DOCTOR

As health care has become increasingly consumer-driven, significant strides have been made throughout the profession to better communicate with consumers. Yet much remains to be done. As an example of the communication hurdles that still exist between patients and their physicians, social workers at major hospitals will often tag along with a doctor when the diagnosis of a chronic or terminal condition is being discussed with the patient—not just to soften the blow but to literally *interpret* for the patient what the doctor is saying.

Article II of the American Hospital Association's Patient Bill of Rights (see Appendix A) states that a patient "…has the right and is encouraged to obtain from physicians and other direct caregivers relevant, current and understandable information concerning diagnosis, treatment and prognosis."

Many doctors and health care workers will take the time to make sure that a patient understands what they are being told about their condition. They will ask a patient if they have any questions, or will pose a question out loud and then answer it, letting the patient know it's okay to ask.

"Now what seems to be the problem?"

Then again, not all doctors will go the extra mile in communicating with a patient, which is why it's critical for patients to be prepared and initiate conversation with their physician.

Doctors Want You to Talk with Them

Let's face it, the doctor is one of the ultimate authority figures in our society. Few people command as much respect as a doctor, save perhaps a priest. And like a priest, the doctor has long been seen as a father-figure, beyond question and above reproach. This perception has evolved over hundreds of years, and its presence is still widespread today. Even a heady consumer-driven market isn't enough to overcome our fears of *daring* to open our mouths in the examination room…unless the doctor is holding a tongue depressor and asking us to "Say ahhhhh."

But the good news, believe it or not, is that doctors *want* you to talk with them. A patient who is prepared to ask questions and share information is a *good* patient. When done properly, this doesn't offend a good doctor, but actually helps him.

Remember, one of the few things doctors don't learn in med school is mind reading. They are doctors, not psychics. Though doctors can run battery after battery of tests on you, as useful as that information is, it's no substitute for letting them know exactly what's bothering you: where it hurts, how much it hurts and how often it hurts. At the same time, a doctor's diagnosis that is laden with complex medical terminology does little to ease your fears about what's wrong and what's happening with your body.

So when you are waiting for your doctor in the examination room, use those few extra quiet moments to collect your thoughts (instead of browsing through the office copy of *Field & Stream* or *Cosmo*), and make a mental list of things *you'd* like to know. Focus on what you are concerned about, and visualize yourself asking the doctor these questions.

Chances are that you've known your doctor for awhile and may already have a more casual, conversational relationship with him. But if not, there's no time like the present to start one.

Think Like a Boy Scout: Be Prepared

Surprisingly, many people find themselves in an examination room answering their doctor's questions with a lot of vague replies like "I'm not sure," "Every so often," "A little bit," "Sort of" and more. Can you imagine if your doctor responded to your questions in the same manner?

"Hey doc, is it serious?"

"Well, sort of."

"Will I be able to go back to work?"

"I'm not sure."

"How long will I have to endure this pain?"

"That depends."

Get the picture? It's important that you are reasonably prepared by the time you sit down in that examination room. Don't hesitate to take notes at home and bring them with you to the doctor's office. The doctor won't mind—again, specific information is going to assist him in helping you. A doctor's office can be slightly intimidating, plus you're obviously not feeling well when you are there, so having it down on paper right in front of you will help ensure that you won't forget to tell him everything you want to say.

Specifically, you'll want to write down as much information as possible about your symptoms. What's bothering you? How is it bothering you? Sharp pains, dull aches, burning sensations? What time do they strike? How often? Where? Are you taking medication now? What type of medication? What are you taking it for? Are you taking it as prescribed? If not, why not?

These may seem like common sense questions that should be easy to answer off the top of your head, but the fact remains that many of us end up in the doctor's office answering questions far less accurately than we could have had we been a little more prepared.

If you are seeing a doctor who you haven't worked with

before and you are on medication, it's important that you inform him of the medication that you are presently taking. He'll probably ask, but you should be prepared to raise the issue in the event that he doesn't. Add a list of your medications to your notebook along with the questions and other information that you have for him. Better yet, bring the medication with you, which will allow him to look at what you are taking. The bottle will tell him more than you can, particularly when it comes to dosages.

WORK AS YOUR DOCTOR'S PARTNER

Your doctor is going to appear a lot less intimidating to you (and visits to his office will be a lot less stressful) if you start to look at him more as your partner than as your manager. Consider him more of a trainer than a coach, someone you consult and work with to get yourself into the best shape as possible, all the while knowing that you are calling the shots (based on his advice). Remember, too, that you are ultimately the one responsible for your own health.

Of course, few of us ever start off with this sort of "partner" relationship with our doctors; it is not something that happens overnight. You don't walk into your doctor's office one afternoon, stick out your hand and exclaim "Hey partner!" It is best to develop this relationship gradually. Every time you are going to the doctor, be prepared. Have this goal of partnership in mind. Think of at least three to five questions you'd like to ask him, jot them down in your notebook and don't talk yourself out of asking them! This is dialog building and it's important. Sure, your doctor may be surprised that you're not sitting there like a "Silent Sam," but he's apt to be pleased. If you feel like it, even let him know that you are determined to take a more proactive role in your health care and that you are looking forward to working with him as a more responsible patient. Encourage him to share more information with you whenever possible. *Let him know that you want to know.* As this pattern continues over the weeks, days, months and years, your doctor will grow used to your active participation. The partnership will grow, becoming stronger and more effective.

If your doctor has a tendency to use a lot of medical terminology that you don't understand, let him know that you have a tough time understanding him when he uses that jargon. Ask him to explain things without such terminology.

Also, remember that while talking with your doctor is a lot easier than you might think, it still requires common conversational etiquette. When you ask your doctor a question, give him time to answer and let him finish a thought or sentence before you ask another. If you are asking him why he wants a series of tests done, or why he has recommended a certain treatment plan for you, or how much the tests or treatments will cost (all very good questions), make sure you do so in a non-confrontational manner. Sometimes we can pose a question in an accusatory or skeptical tone without meaning to, so it's important to be aware of how a question may come out. Try framing it like this: "I'm eager to know if this particular treatment will affect me differently than other treatments. What can I expect?"

QUESTIONS TO ASK

Try to ask relevant questions, and don't worry about sounding dumb. As the old saying goes, "The only stupid questions are the ones you don't ask." This is especially important if you have concerns about a treatment or test your doctor has prescribed. Consider asking your doctor these questions:

- ▸ Why do I need this test or this treatment?

- ▸ How does the test/treatment work?

- ▸ What will the test tell us?

- ▸ How soon will the treatment start working?

- ▸ What will the treatment do for me, specifically?

- ▸ What happens if I decline to undergo the treatment or test?

- ▸ What are the specific alternatives? Why weren't those chosen first?

If you don't like or don't feel entirely comfortable about the answers you hear, let your doctor know that you'd like more information. Asking for a second opinion is not heresy! You may think that your doctor is going to feel as if you are going "behind his back" in asking for a second opinion, when in fact your doctor is quite unlikely to feel threatened by your request. It will probably reaffirm his perception of you as an engaged patient and self-advocate. However, if you can't bring yourself to tell your doctor that you'd like a second opinion, then don't. There's no law that says you have to, it just makes good sense to do so if you are trying to cultivate an active partnership with him.

PERSONAL QUESTIONS? SHOOT!

Most of us cringe when we think about having to talk with our doctor (or nurse) about personal matters such as sex and using the bathroom. I remember that the first time a nurse asked me what color my stool was, I told her I didn't have a stool. She smiled and rephrased the question.

A college buddy of mine was once infected with gonorrhea, a well-known type of sexually transmitted disease (STD). He knew he was in trouble, but was literally paralyzed by the dual social hammers of shame and embarrassment. This sort of reluctance to seek treatment for STDs is common and potentially quite dangerous. Left untreated, certain STDs can cause extreme health problems, leading to sterility and in some instances death. If the thought of his family's doctor inspecting his genitals didn't scare him enough, the worry that the doctor would promptly call his parents to "report him" kept him from getting treated for more than a week after he discovered "something was wrong down there." He finally overcame his embarrassment and sought help at a local clinic.

Like my friend, most people have a difficult time discussing any aspect of sex with their physician. They are worried about what their doctor will think of them or, worse, who their doctor might tell (such as my friend's concern that the doctor would call his folks).

It is important to realize that doctors are not there to hand down a moral judgment. They are there to help you get well and maintain your health. If your doctor knows you well, don't be surprised if he offers you some friendly advice about how to avoid repeating such an unpleasant experience. But the chances are slim to none that he'll launch into a sermon in the examining room.

More importantly, by the time he's in that examining room, your doctor has seen every body part there is to see a thousand times over. Quite simply, "a body part is a body part is a body part." Remembering this simple fact can make it easier for you if you ever need to talk about a potentially embarrassing problem. They've heard it all and they've seen it all—and that's good news for you.

SPECIALISTS

During the course of the examination, your doctor may refer you to another physician. There may be several reasons he wants you to be examined by another doctor. He may want a second opinion to bolster his own diagnosis or to offer him an alternative theory. He may have a solid diagnosis, but wants a specialist in that area to examine and treat you for the condition.

Whatever his reason, you should ask your doctor why he is making the referral. Ask your doctor if the physician he is referring you to is a specialist with a lot of experience with your specific medical condition. Ask your doctor if he will still be the one coordinating your care through the specialist and, if so, how exactly that will work.

CHAPTER 3

Alternative and Complementary Medicine: Remedy or Ruse?

"The part can never be well unless the whole is well…This is the great error of our day in the treatment of the human body, that the physicians separate the soul from the body."

PLATO, CHARMIDES

 When most people think of health care in this country, they probably still envision the icon of Western medicine: the doctor with a private practice and privileges at the local 300-bed hospital. Certainly, this world still

exists and, in some areas, continues to dominate. But even as traditional Western medicine continues to undergo changes in our country, a whole other world of medicine and therapeutic treatments is emerging and gaining widespread acceptance in mainstream American society.

Chances are that you've probably heard the terms "alternative medicine" and "complementary medicine" bandied about in conversation or on the news. It's also probably just as likely that you, like most Americans, aren't really too sure what exactly alternative or complementary medicine is, who practices it and which illnesses are treated by it.

ALTERNATIVE MEDICINE: WHAT IS IT?

At its essence, alternative medicine is a very broad term used to describe myriad treatments that fall outside of traditional Western medical practices. Since the term "alternative" sometimes has a negative connotation, proponents of alternative treatments often use the term "complementary medicine" instead. The terms refer to the same group of practices and will be used interchangeably throughout this chapter.

The National Institute of Health's Office of Alternative Medicine classifies alternative medicine as, "An unrelated group of non-orthodox therapeutic practices, which often have explanatory systems that do not follow conventional biomedical explanations."

Others describe complementary medicine as "medical interventions not taught in the United States."

Most Americans are familiar with the ancient Chinese

practice of acupuncture or the chiropractic treatment of back disorders. These are two popular forms of alternative medicine that have grown considerably in this country and have garnered some grudging respect from the medical establishment.

But complementary medicine goes far beyond acupuncture and chiropractic. It stretches along a broad continuum of treatments—from the down-to-earth to the very far-out—for almost every sort of malady you can imagine. Folk medicine, herbal medicine, energy medicine, diets, shark cartilage, New Age therapies, music therapy and massage therapy are just a few points on the tip of this very big iceberg.

To give you an idea of just how broad the spectrum of alternative medicine is, consider that some people who keep a balanced diet and meditate say they are practicing complementary medicine. Others who drink and bathe in urine also say they are practicing alternative medicine.

No matter who says their practicing it, the fact is that millions of Americans today are spending billions of dollars—yes, *billions*—on alternative medicine every year.

Dr. George Ulett, a clinical professor of Community and Family Medicine at the St. Louis University School of Medicine, likens alternative medicine in America today to a giant garage sale. "Most of it is junk," Ulett says. "But if you look around long enough, you're going to find a few gems that you can take home, clean up and put to good use."

Ulett studied acupuncture in China during the 1960s and recently authored *Alternative Medicine or Magic Healing: The Trick is to Know the Difference*—a book that focuses exclusively on complementary medicine.

Highlighting the impact that alternative medicine is making in America, Ulett notes that a third of all medical patients in the nation today seek some form of complementary medicine, either in conjunction with traditional treatment or as their primary form of treatment.

While the scope of alternative medicine in our society is indisputable, there is great debate as to whether or not the growth of complementary medicine is, in fact, a good thing. Some traditional doctors accuse practitioners of alternative medicine of being quacks and frauds, while some practitioners of complementary medicine dub the traditional American medical establishment the "Medical Mafia."

Despite all the high-octane hyperbole, it's safe to say that opinions among reasonable people vary greatly, depending on the specific alternative treatment and what it is being used to cure.

"People are often looking for a 'miracle cure' to one affliction or illness or another," Ulett says. "People with chronic illnesses are often desperate and vulnerable. The elderly are vulnerable. There's no medical cure for aging or arthritis, and so some of these 'herbologists' have a field day advertising herbs that allegedly cure all of the above."

This chapter is meant to give you a basic understanding of some the alternative treatments that are available in the United States today, as well as some of the treatments that Americans have been seeking out in other parts of the world. The purpose is not to pass a medical or therapeutic judgment on any of the particular alternative treatments that are listed, but to simply make you aware of the options available.

Perhaps the most important thing to remember when

you are considering an alternative form of medical treatment is that you should consult with your primary physician along the way. The Burton Goldberg Group's vast *Alternative Medicine: The Definitive Guide* notes that many of the methods of alternative medicine have not been investigated or approved by the Federal Drug Administration or other regulatory agencies and that national, state and local laws may pertain to certain practices. Again, check with your doctor or another licensed health professional before embarking on any experimental treatment. Don't be embarrassed or shy about the fact that you are considering complementary medicine as a treatment option. You have that right and your doctor should not be upset with you for considering it. He or she will probably be glad that you sought out his or her advice on the matter, because that means you're thinking about all of your options carefully. At the same time, don't brush off your doctor's advice if he warns against pursuing a particular form of complementary medicine. Ask your doctor to explain his concerns about the particular treatment to you. Don't hesitate to seek additional input from other physicians, as second, third and even fourth opinions can be helpful.

WHERE IS ALTERNATIVE MEDICINE DELIVERED?

In many cases, hospitals have doctors who use forms of alternative medicine along with traditional treatment therapies. In such instances, complementary medicine may be delivered in the standard hospital setting. In most other

"Take 3 of these and call me in the morning."

cases, complementary medicine is delivered through clinics, wellness centers and other locations that are less clinical than the traditional hospital setting.

VARIOUS TYPES OF ALTERNATIVE TREATMENTS

If you log on the internet and surf the world wide web under "Alternative Medicine," you'll get a better understanding of just how many different types of complementary medicine are being practiced today. Or pick up a copy of *Alternative Medicine: A Definitive Guide*, which explores a vast array of complementary therapies and the health conditions to which they are applied.

Listed below are some of the more common—and some of the more controversial—types of alternative medicine:

Acupuncture This ancient Chinese medical practice, which dates back 5,000 years, is based on the belief that an ill person's life force—also known as "chi"—is out of balance. Practitioners of acupuncture believe that a person's chi flows along specific paths across the body. To restore the balance of the chi and regain health, needles are inserted into a variety of points on the body (there are more than 1,000 such points, though only a dozen are usually used), which helps redirect the person's life energy along the right path. Acupuncture is used to treat a wide array of illnesses and injuries, as well as to alleviate pain. According to Dr. Ulett, there are about 10,000 acupuncturists in the United States today, nearly a third of whom are MDs or DOs (Doctor of Osteopathy). Approximately 85% of acupuncturists practice traditional acupuncture, which employs needles. A growing number of acupuncturists are using electrodes instead of needles to stimulate the body points.

Aromatherapy A type of herbal medicine, aromatherapy uses oils extracted from plants and herbs to treat a wide array of medical conditions. The oils used in aromatherapy can be applied in different ways, including inhaling and topical applications on the skin.

Auriculotherapy Essentially acupuncture of the ear. There are 30 basic points on the ear that practitioners believe can be manipulated in the same manner that acupuncture points can be manipulated on the body. Again, practitioners can use either needles or electro probes. Auriculotherapy is used to treat pain, dyslexia and other functional imbalances. Proponents of the therapy also apply it in treating alcohol, cigarette and drug addiction.

Bodywork A broad genre of treatments that includes massage therapy, reflexology, movement awareness and energy balancing which is used to improve a person's overall health as well as specific injuries and illnesses. As the Burton Goldberg Group's alternative medicine bible notes, there are literally hundreds of therapies that fall under the bodywork category, some styles of which are even practiced under trademarked names.

▸ Reportedly older than its cousin acupuncture, *acupressure* uses physical stimulation of the same points along the body rather than needles. Unlike acupuncture, self-acupressure techniques can be taught for people to apply to themselves.

▸ *Massage therapy* has been practiced for thousands of years, perhaps most commonly as a stress reliever. Today, massage therapy is used to treat a wide range of afflictions, from whiplash to various diseases.

▸ *Reflexology* is based on the premise that by stimulating certain areas on the hands and feet, therapists can effect corresponding areas all over the body. Like massage therapy, reflexology is used to reduce stress, improve the blood supply and help restore balance to the body. Reflexology is used to treat a variety of maladies. One recent headline in an alternative medicine journal boasted "Subdue PMS with Your Feet!"

▸ *Polarity Therapy* is also based on the concept of body energy and utilizes the stimulation of pressure points and joints. It incorporates other therapies, such as hydrotherapy and reflexology, in order to restore the balance and flow of the body's energy.

Cell Therapy This treatment involves the injection of healthy cells into the body. It is used to stimulate healing and treat degenerative diseases such as Parkinson's disease, arthritis and cancer. Though used in other parts of the world, cell therapy is not approved for use in the United States.

Chiropractic The granddaddy of alternative medicine in America, surpassing even acupuncture. Though practiced in many forms by civilizations dating back to the ancient Egyptians, chiropractic medicine was introduced to the United States in the late 1800s and is now the second largest primary health care field in the world. Chiropractic means "of the hands" and chiropractors specialize in working with bones, joints and the spinal cord. They are commonly sought out to treat lower back pain. The basic concept behind chiropractic medicine is that by manipulating the spine and joints, chiropractors can change the nervous system—which in turn results in improved health. Once derided as quacks, there are now 50,000 licensed chiropractors practicing in the United States. Chiropractors must undergo four years of specialized education before being licensed. According to Dr. Ulett, approximately half of the chiropractors in this country also employ acupuncture in their practice. Some chiropractors use the practice to treat an array of injuries and ailments, including drug addiction.

Colon Therapy Colon therapy is the process of flushing out the colon, a large section of the lower intestine, in order to remove excess fecal build up. Implementing this "super enema" can last as long as 45 minutes, during which as many as six liters of purified water are flushed in and out, cleaning the entire five feet of the colon. By contrast, a standard enema cleans 8 to 12 inches. Practitioners of colon therapy prescribe it for an assortment of medical problems, including headaches, bad breath, lung congestion and fatigue. If you are seeking colon therapy, it is extremely important that you find a certified and well-kept facility.

Craniosacral Therapy The manipulation of the skull to treat everything from headaches to strokes.

Detoxification Therapy Essentially the process of ridding your body of all the chemicals you ingest daily, intentionally or otherwise, including pesticides, food preservatives and recreational and prescription drugs. While there are various forms of detoxification therapy, including colon therapy, the general process usually includes dieting and fasting. Those who prescribe detoxification therapy note that extreme caution must be taken when undergoing the treatment. They stress that it should be administered by a qualified health professional.

Energy Medicine (Biofeedback) Based on monitoring electromagnetic frequencies emitted by the body in order to diagnose a present illness or predict a future one. Treatments are applied with hi-tech instruments designed to restore the body's energy balance.

Flower Therapy Pioneered by an English physician during the 1930s, flower therapy focuses on the role that emotions play in our health. Flower-based remedies are directed at a person's emotional state as a means to improve their overall well-being. The remedies use 38 different types of flowering plants and trees that are believed to have an effect on one's psychological state.

Herbal Medicine An ancient form of medicine that has been applied by almost every culture on the planet, playing a role in traditional Chinese, Indian and Western medicine. In its broader sense, herbal medicine is essentially the nature-based equivalent of chemical medicine, using the active components found in plants to treat illnesses and improve health rather than synthetic compounds. Herbal medicine is practiced throughout the world today and has been used to treat everything from PMS to AIDS.

Homeopathy Founded in the late 18th century, homeopathy is a system of non-toxic medicine that is used to treat everything from lupus to the common cold. It is recognized and regulated in the United States, where there are an estimated 3,000 practitioners.

Hydrotherapy The application of hot and cold temperatures, through water, ice and steam, to treat a host of maladies and improve circulation. Therapies include salt rubs, whirlpools, saunas, ice packs and more.

Hypnotherapy (Hypnosis) Mind over matter. Or, in this case, mind over body. "Your mind is a key player in any illness and any chance of recovery," says Dr. O.T. Bonnett, the author of *Confessions of a Healer: The Truth from an Unconventional Family Doctor*. Bonnett notes that he uses hypnosis in his practice and advocates it in the treatment of heart disease, cancer, asthma, arthritis and a host of other ills. Dr. Bonnett, and others who employ hypnosis as a medical treatment, argue that the human body is constantly constructed according to the thoughts and the beliefs of the mind. Accordingly, by manipulating the mind you can change the course of the body and restore health. Dr. Ulett notes that the American Medical Association recognizes hypnosis as a "useful adjunct" treatment to other medicine when working on pain management. He notes that the practice of hypnosis is not as popular as it could be, in part because it is time-consuming. "People expect everything today to get done 'Bang! Bang! Bang!' and hypnosis takes time."

Laetrile Illegal in the United States, Laetrile is a non-toxic substance—primarily vitamin B17—derived from apricot pits that is used to treat cancer patients, often in conjunction with other vitamin-based therapies. Laetrile is available in Mexico and thousands of Americans have sought treatment south of the border.

Yoga Yoga is often practiced in connection with Hinduism. Meaning "union," yoga uses meditation (restraint of breath, repression of activity, withdrawal of the senses) to elevate the mind to a higher plane or state of being. Like acupuncture, Yoga is centered on the concept of body energy. Practitioners report lower levels of stress and a heightened sense of well-being.

Urine Therapy Practitioners of urine therapy believe that urea, an active component of urine, offers a wide variety of beneficial health applications. The premise of urine therapy is that people who don't chemically interfere with their body's natural cycle (by eating foods laden with chemicals, for instance) produce urine that is harmless, healthy and nutritional. Proponents believe that urine, when ingested or rubbed into the skin, purifies the blood and tissues, provides useful nutrients and helps the body determine what elements are out of balance. It is prescribed for everything from a sore throat to skin cancer.

Again, these are just a few types of alternative or complementary medicine—literally just blips on a vast screen.

According to Dr. Ulett, if you have decided to explore an alternative treatment for any kind of injury or illness, you should consult your doctor first. It is very important to make sure you know exactly what is ailing you before you seek an alternative form of medical treatment. Ulett advises patients to let a traditional doctor establish a diagnosis before considering alternative treatments. "Make sure what you have isn't going to kill you if it's not treated traditionally," he says. "Make sure those bad headaches you think are from stress really aren't caused by a brain tumor. Don't diagnose from alternative medicine."

WHERE TO FIND PROVIDERS OF ALTERNATIVE MEDICINE

The availability of alternative health therapies will obviously vary from community to community. Places like Santa Monica, California, or Santa Fe, New Mexico, or New York City are going to have far more alternative medicine options than other parts of the country. A great place to start looking in any community is the local yellow pages. Look under the name of the specific treatment you are considering.

If your community has an "underground" or alternative press, that's a good place to check as well. If a community has an active alternative health scene, chances are good that there will be one or more publications that cater exclusively to it, such as *The Whole Person*, which circulates throughout Los Angeles County. These publications often include calendars for free events and workshops, and usually include many advertisements from local practitioners.

Don't be afraid to ask your doctor either; remember, they should be involved in this process.

The American Hospital: A Brief History

"I think it frets the saints in heaven to see
How many desolate creatures on Earth
Have learnt the simple dues of fellowship
And social comfort, in a hospital"

ELIZABETH BARRETT BROWNING

 Icons of America's power and wealth, hospitals are interwoven through the fabric of our nation, providing the backbone to the largest and most sophisticated health care system in the industrial world.

According to a recent study by the American Hospital Association, there are nearly 6,300 hospitals in the United

States, ranging in size from tiny 20-bed community hospitals in the rural heartland to thousand-bed mammoths that serve the major urban population centers.

The significance of the role the traditional hospital continues to play in America is reflected by some of the statistics the AHA has published. In a typical year, more than 33 million Americans are admitted to the hospital for a total of nearly 260 million inpatient days. On any given day, there are more than 700,000 Americans in the hospital.

Over 24 million Americans undergo surgery each year, with almost half of these requiring an inpatient stay at the hospital. At the same time, outpatient hospital care is booming. Americans use outpatient hospital services nearly 500 million times a year, including almost 100 million trips to emergency rooms across the nation.

The heavy-hitting role that hospitals play in the economy cannot be overstated. Hospitals employ more than 4 million Americans and spend more than $320 billion dollars. Whew!

While those numbers make it clear that hospitals still play a massive and vital part in the health care system we use today, the future of hospitals as we now know them—if not in doubt—is clearly in flux. As costs spiraled during the 1970s and early '80s, managed care began to take root in various regions. With its aggressive focus on containing costs, managed care has helped redefine the American hospital, for better *and* worse.

Today, the health care system that only a decade ago prided itself on massive hospitals with hundreds or thousands of beds and extensive inpatient care no longer exists.

Large hospitals that once boasted thriving patient censuses now look more like beached whales, with entire wings shuttered and beds (once the omnipotent indicator of market strength and community relevance) collecting little more than dust. As the length of inpatient stays continues to decline, outpatient care continues to grow.

I recently rode the elevator up to the sixth floor of a major regional medical center in Southern California while researching this book. Stepping out with the doctor who was giving me a tour, we gazed down a long hall into a wing that had been "deactivated." What we saw was an empty, dusty nursing station and rows and rows of empty rooms, all fallen deathly silent like some sort of medical ghost town. It was eerie.

As we consider how we use hospitals today and how we may well use them tomorrow, we should take a moment to consider how we used them as a nation through the years gone by.

Hospitals in America predate the Revolution and the birth of the Republic. In fact, they first appeared on the North American continent shortly after the Spanish explorer Cortez conquered the New World. He founded a hospital in Mexico City in 1527, an institution that still stands to this day (albeit under a different name).

The French followed soon after, establishing hospitals in what today is Canada. In the mid-1600s, several houses in what is now New York City were turned into a hospital for, interestingly enough, soldiers and slaves. It would be more than a hundred years before civilians were treated there.

In the King's England, there were two types of hospitals:

Royal Hospitals and Voluntary Hospitals, the latter de-signed for use by the common man. They were called voluntary because they were staffed by volunteers, unlike the paid physicians at the Royal Hospitals, and survived on contributions from the elite—who generally funded the hospitals as a philanthropic endeavor or out of a feeling of religious duty.

The concept of the Voluntary Hospital was established in America as the colonies grew. There were three early hospitals in America that were very important: Pennsylvania Hospital (in Philadelphia), New York Hospital and Massachusetts General Hospital in Boston.

Established by Quaker doctors, Philadelphia Hospital was the biggest hospital of its time and was the first to be used extensively by civilians. When it opened in a rented house in 1752, its staff of three doctors and a nurse could handle about two dozen patients at any one time.

"I hear they have the top radiologist in the country."

By the early 1700s the hospital had moved into its own building with a much larger capacity, but its patient population continued to swell as a result of the fact that early American hospitals also treated the mentally ill. It's reported that during the early years of Pennsylvania Hospital, roughly one-third of its patients suffered from mental illness.

Unfortunately, the mentally ill were treated horrendously during that early era. The patients, known simply as "lunatics" by both medical staff and society at large, were subjected to the twisted voyeurism of the general public. The cash-short hospital would, for an admission fee, allow people to come in off the street and gawk at the mental patients and taunt them as they languished in their dank wards. Such an inhumane and ugly policy is hard to believe by current hospital standards. Modern hospitals won't even confirm if a particular person has been admitted without permission from the patient.

Like almost every other aspect of life in the colonies, the Revolutionary War placed a great burden on the developing hospitals, which had to treat both American and British soldiers. For Pennsylvania Hospital, the war was particularly difficult since it was founded by Quakers, a passive religious group who were essentially loyal to the crown. With the revolutionary government seated in the colony, tensions were high and funding to the hospital was cut.

Medicine was developing rapidly by then (as it is now), but the standard of care in those early hospitals—while probably top notch for the time—would likely terrify any one of us if we were admitted.

By the early 1800s, Pennsylvania Hospital had a surgical

ward for amputations and the resetting of broken bones. Remember that anesthesia had not yet been developed and infections were common. The practices of bleeding and purging were still commonly employed.

At the same time, various features of the modern hospital were beginning to appear. In the late 1700s, the Pennsylvania Hospital offered outpatient services that treated hundreds of patients. They eventually built a separate outpatient clinic.

While hospitals developed in the established population centers on the East Coast, they also spread with the westward migration of colonists, popping up along the Mississippi River. One of the first hospitals west of that great river was established in St. Louis in the late 1820s by the city's Catholic bishop. The hospital was located in a three-room log cabin donated by an Irish-American trader.

Times on the frontier were rough and hospitals, like the one in St. Louis, often saw the worst of it. There were cholera outbreaks, deadly epidemics that wiped out large swaths of the population. In 1849, a cholera outbreak killed almost nine percent of the entire city. The hospital filled with thousands of suffering patients, nearly half of whom died. Many hospital staff members were also infected during the tragic episode, adding to the number of casualties.

Karen Wolf, a registered nurse who has studied the evolution of hospitals and nursing in America, says the first big hospital boom hit after the Civil War and continued through the turn of the century. The growing availability of nursing labor and the rise of the philanthropic movement converged to meet the needs of the hundreds of thousands of casualties left in the wake of the Civil War.

As the nation evolved from an agricultural society to an industrial powerhouse, the role and the scope of the hospital continued to grow. Textile towns that boasted huge labor pools needed adequate facilities to keep the workers healthy—at least healthy enough to keep working the mills. Hospitals became vital cogs in the machine that kept the urban population centers running.

By the early 1920s, historians estimate there were nearly 5,000 hospitals in the United States, with the majority of them being general hospitals. Most cities and towns of any size had a hospital. Hospitals were no longer just the place where people who couldn't afford health care went for treatment. With the advent of new technology and a more professional staff, people who could afford to have a doctor pay them a house visit were now starting to utilize the hospital.

Surgery also became a central component of a hospital's function during this era. While the house call and office visit were still where many Americans received their medical care, surgery was now conducted almost exclusively at hospitals. Historians note that it was at this point that costs began to climb dramatically, as the hospital became a major capital investment. In addition, government regulation of hospitals became a priority during the 1920s.

Insurance came into play in the 1930s, Wolf says, in order to help hospitals deal with the financial hits they had taken during the depression. In 1934, the New York United Hospital Fund was created with the help of the American Hospital Association, which essentially put into practice the concept of prepaid hospital care. By 1938, Wolf notes, nearly a million and a half Americans had enrolled in Blue Cross plans.

World War II fueled the next big changes in hospitals, as the government helped fast-track women into nursing. Wolf notes that college-educated women were first drawn into nursing during the war, which significantly changed the profession. Historically, nursing had attracted women who couldn't afford to go to college.

Following the end of the war, Congress passed the Hill/Burton Act, which marked a massive infusion of government money into the building of hospitals and the number of beds available. The impact of this legislation could be felt through the 1970s.

During the 1950s, hospital care continued to evolve by leaps and bounds, as rapid advances were made in medical technology. Radiology, antibiotics and the use of plastic all changed the shape of hospital care.

It has been said that, in some respects, hospitals in America took on the same characteristics as the defense industry, particularly during the height of the Cold War in the 1970s and early '80s. Building boomed. The bigger the better. The concept of "If you build it, they will come" ruled. Cost seemed no object.

Other factors came to bear on hospitals during this time. The social flux created by the women's movement, the disability rights movement and the environmental movement all played a role in shaping hospital care.

Today, as in the defense industry, the bubble has clearly burst. The boom years are over. But also like defense, America still has one of the most complex and well-kept health systems in the world.

Hospitals: Check 'em Out Before Checking In

"It may seem a strange principle to enunciate as the very first requirement in a hospital that it should do the sick no harm."

FLORENCE NIGHTINGALE

Being admitted to a hospital today for non-emergency medical procedures has radically changed in many respects during the past ten years. One of the most significant changes for consumers has been the shifting of many hospital services to outpatient care, which has resulted in shorter stays at the hospital for fewer people.

Managed care and advances in technology have combined to cut the length of stays. Remember the episode of *I Love Lucy* that features Lucy giving birth to Little Ricky? When Lucy starts to go into labor, Desi Arnaz races out of the bedroom with a suitcase or two, obviously pre-packed for the trip to the hospital. Back then, in the 1950s, the Lucy Ricardos of America might indeed find themselves getting plenty of R&R at the hospital after delivery, thus needing a couple of suitcases full of clothes, needlework, magazines, stationery, make-up, etc.

Today, the same sitcom scene, if accurate, would feature Ricky racing out of the bedroom with a camcorder and maybe a knapsack. Chances are that Lucy would deliver Little Ricky and be back home the following night in time to catch the *Tonight Show*. And that's presuming she didn't skip the hospital completely and have the baby at home.

What hospital you go to for a non-emergency procedure will depend in part on where your doctor has privileges. With the exception of "teaching hospitals," which tend to be large medical centers, most hospitals do not have staff doctors. Rather, doctors in the area will receive "privileges" to admit and treat their patients at a hospital. Many doctors have privileges at more than one hospital, while other doctors will use only one hospital. Some hospitals have physicians on duty around the clock, while other smaller hospitals might not. It's important to know if the hospital you'll be staying at has physicians on duty 24 hours-a-day, seven days-a-week.

If you are not tied to a particular physician you may want to shop around for a hospital, which makes sense in today's consumer-driven climate. Costs can vary and the extent of services certainly changes from hospital to hospital.

DIFFERENT KINDS OF HOSPITALS

Medical centers. General hospitals. Community hospitals. Teaching hospitals. Public hospitals. Private hospitals. For-profit hospitals. Non-profit hospitals. Considering all these titles one might get the idea that there are a lot of different kinds of hospitals and, in some regards, there are, though they are all connected by the common thread of providing the best possible medical care for the communities they serve.

The nation's largest hospitals are often classified as "medical centers" and are usually associated with medical schools. Thus, they are also classified as "teaching hospitals." These monoliths have full-time staff physicians (meaning they actually work for the hospital and don't just have admitting privileges) who are usually making rounds 24 hours-a-day. As a result of their size and scope, teaching hospitals often also serve as research centers for the federal government.

Community hospitals are generally smaller operations (though some can still be quite large, with bed space numbering as high as five or six hundred) and are less likely to be teaching hospitals. Community hospitals are run for profit and are therefore managed like a business and are owned either by an individual or actual stockholders.

Even non-profit hospitals today are operated by an administration that closely resembles a corporate management structure. Hospitals are likely to have a Chief Executive Officer (CEO), a President (often the CEO), a Chief Operating Officer (COO), a Chief Financial Officer (CFO), a Board of Directors and a slew of vice presidents who oversee various divisions of the hospital. As a typical health care consumer, it is unlikely that you will need to contact any of the administrators during your hospital stay, though it is important that you understand that non-profit status and philanthropic roots aside, hospitals are big businesses and are operated as such.

A hospital's medical operations also has a variety of management positions, including Medical Director, Director of Nursing, Hospital Administrator, Chief of Staff and various department heads (i.e., Director of Oncology, Director of Maternity and Child Health, etc.). These positions are filled with medical professionals and you, as a consumer, may come in contact with one or more of them. For example, if you are shopping for a hospital in which to deliver your baby and are seeking more specific information than what was provided by the maternity staff or patient services, you may end up contacting the Director of Maternity and Child Health.

Teaching hospitals feature staffs of interns and residents. Interns are doctors who have completed medical school and are in their first year of training at the hospital. Residents are doctors who have finished their internship and have moved on to training in specialized fields of medicine. Teaching hospitals will also feature third- and fourth-year medical school students, who may also participate in your care at the hospital—under the supervision of a doctor.

ACCREDITATION

Every couple of years most hospitals in the United States undergo a process called "accreditation," in which they are inspected and evaluated by a team of independent doctors and nurses. Created by the American Hospital Association, the Joint Commission on Accreditation of Hospitals ensures that national standards of care are maintained. While hospitals are technically not required to undergo accreditation, they can't receive Medicare reimbursements if they are not. Non-accredited teaching hospitals are not recognized and interns and residents will not get credit for training in them.

WHEN SHOPPING FOR A HOSPITAL

Some hospitals specialize in certain kinds of care, such as cardio care (for heart patients) or cancer care. Some hospitals have state-of-the-art surgical units that are staffed by specialists and are better suited for more complex procedures than most other hospitals.

Even if you are in an HMO, like Kaiser, you may have some flexibility to choose among institutions within the organization. Remember, just because a certain hospital is closest to your house doesn't mean it is the best one for you to use. Your primary care doctor will be able to help steer you in the right direction, but make sure that he decides *with* you, not for you. If your doctor has already selected a hospital for you, ask him why he chose that hospital and ask if there are any other alternatives.

Again, the key is to not automatically assume that your doctor has picked the right hospital for you, or that you should use a certain hospital simply because it's within two miles of your house. Investigate and ask questions. If you are considering one hospital over another, don't be shy about asking for some patient references. See if you can find some people who have been treated at the competing hospitals for the same health problem for which you are seeking care and find out what they have to say about their experience.

WHAT TO BRING

While the hospital is not the Hilton, almost all of your basic needs are going to be provided for during your hospital stay. The list of what you *should* bring to the hospital will be easier (and much shorter) to compile if you first consider what you *shouldn't* bring. Each hospital has a check-in list, which is usually contained in their patient handbook, that you can ask for prior to your arrival. However, common sense will go a long way in saving you hassle and embarrassment during the check-in process.

The rule of thumb when considering what to bring with you should be "Will I really need this item while at the hospital?" and "Will I really use this item while at the hospital?"

Keep It Simple

As a result of stringent electrical safety and fire standards, electrical appliances like hair dryers, shavers, plug-in radios and televisions are not allowed. Battery-operated versions of these appliances might be, but you need to check first before you start packing.

Remember that most hospital rooms are equipped with television sets and even radios, so trying to bring those will probably be excessive. Some hospitals even offer video games via the television sets to their patients. To help you pass the time—as hospital stays can turn into marathons of excruciating boredom if they are prolonged—you may consider bringing some reading material or a Walkman with books-on-tape. The hospital gift shop is likely to carry a selection of magazines and daily newspapers as well. But be realistic: Don't bring a library or a music collection when you are going to be in the hospital for two or three days.

Personal effects are important to bring. While razors, deodorant, toothpaste and more are probably all available at the hospital, you may be charged if they provide it for you—plus you won't get to choose the kind you like.

Pillows and blankets will be provided by the hospital. If you absolutely can't sleep without your lucky pillow or magic comforter, then you may want to bring those with you. If you do bring such items, be sure to visibly mark them with tags that identify them as your personal items, lest the facilities staff mistake them for hospital issue and remove them during the daily linen change. If that happens, you can kiss your lucky blanket goodbye.

For a planned hospital stay, leave your valuables at home! You are not going to impress the hospital staff with jewelry or a wad of bills in your wallet and you may be putting yourself unnecessarily at risk by bringing such things. *Hospitals are not responsible for your personal possessions!* They will make this clear to you during the admissions process. Amazingly, many patients still bring personal valuables with them. Do so at your own risk!

If you find yourself in a hospital with valuables on you, inquire whether the hospital has a safe deposit box available for patients—as many hospitals do. If you have an excessive amount of cash on you (probably anything over $40), ask about having that safeguarded as well, especially if sending it back home with a relative or friend is not an option. Some hospitals will convert the cash into a check from the hospital which they will give to you upon discharge. Again, ask the nurse or a representative from the patient services department as soon as possible. While hospitals are generally extremely safe places with very trustworthy staff members, be realistic. Crime is everywhere. Better to be safe than sorry.

YOUR ROOM

There are still two basic kinds of rooms in most hospitals today: private and semi-private. Don't let the titles fool you. There is nothing truly private about anything in a hospital, except perhaps a grieving room where a family can go to after a loved one dies or a bathroom with a lock on the door.

Considering their mission, hospitals rely upon constant observation and monitoring of patients, which means that a steady stream of doctors, nurses and other members of the hospital staff will be moving through your room on a regular basis. Add visitors to that and it may seem like you can't get any rest, though of course you can end the visitations by asking the charge nurse to turn them away until you feel more up to receiving them.

Private vs. Semi-Private

The real difference between a private and a semi-private room is the number of beds. A private room has a single bed, so you will be the only patient being treated in the room. A semi-private room is a room that has two or more beds (usually two, sometimes four and occasionally as many as six), with the "semi" being the floor-to-ceiling curtains that can be circled around your bed to affect visual privacy (which can be nice when it comes to bath time or the bed pan).

Single Rooms

Single-bed rooms are usually reserved for patients who have a contagious infection, though they can be used by others as well. If you know you will be checking into a hospital on a particular date, call your doctor's office and ask if he can reserve a private room for you, or call the hospital directly. If their single rooms are all occupied when you are admitted, you will get a multi-bed room. But you may find that you can transfer to a single-bed room as soon as one opens up—if you have requested one in advance.

Before doing so, however, you may want to check your insurance policy to see if it will cover the cost of a single-bed room, which are often more expensive than a multi-bed room. If a single-bed room is medically required, your insurance will almost certainly pay for it. If it's not required and you use one by choice, you may be held accountable for the difference. The hospital may be willing to give you a single-bed room at the same price, especially if the census is low and they have rooms to spare. However, it is critical that you establish this up front, before you arrive at the hospital to check in. A hospital's patient services department is a good place to start when researching your options.

A word about the bed in your room: most hospitals use beds that are higher and more narrow than most standard beds at home. Many of them are also electrically operated, so your nurse will probably show you how to work the bed (such as adjusting elevation and position) once you are assigned a room. The bed is also likely to have safety rails around it to prevent you from falling out.

FOOD

There's good news and bad news when it comes to hospital food. The good news is that hospitals today are boasting a greater variety of food for its patients that is much better than their reputations would allow. The bad news is that no one has ever gone to hospitals for the food and that hasn't changed. No matter how you slice it, hospital food still (in most cases) consists of mass-produced, cafeteria-style meals.

Hospitals employ dietitians and nutritionists who work closely with your doctor to meet your nutritional needs during your hospital stay. Accordingly, you may want a double cheeseburger (and hospitals do have them), but you may end up with puréed veggies instead.

What many people don't understand is that while hospitals generally have set menus each day (sometimes offering patients several choices per meal), you can make special requests or independent orders, if your doctor allows it. My last day in the hospital I asked for—and got—a cheeseburger and strawberry shake.

Major hospitals also have cafeterias and coffee shops that are open 24 hours for families, friends and staff.

VISITORS

Visiting hours and policies—and the strictness with which they are enforced—will vary from hospital to hospital and from unit to unit. For example, the intensive care unit will have very narrow guidelines for visitors that are strictly enforced, while a standard recovery room will have a much broader policy that is likely to be more lenient. You should find out the hospital's policy when you check in so that you can avoid inconveniencing family members and friends who discover they can't see you. Hours may also change from day-to-day.

In almost all instances, hospitals prefer (if not require) visitors to check in before walking into a patient's room.

Most hospitals will usually limit the number of people allowed in a room at any given time to between three and five. There are practical reasons for this, as nurses can't do their jobs effectively if there are 15 people jammed into one room at the same time.

Immediate family members, which are usually considered to be spouses, children, parents, grandparents and grandchildren or a patient-identified support person, have 24-hour access to a loved one in some hospitals.

While hospitals welcome children as visitors, you should expect to have them with an adult guardian at all times if they are under 12-years-old. A big hospital is like a self-contained city and it doesn't take much for a child to get lost.

Keep in mind that visiting can be limited or even canceled completely by the patient, the doctor or nursing staff at any time, especially if rules are not being followed.

SECURITY

Most hospitals today are equipped with professional security services, to one degree or another. Smaller hospitals may have a lone security guard on the premises who has been contracted out from a private firm, while the big urban hospitals have their own mini-police forces who are responsible for ensuring the safety of patients, staff and visitors in all areas of the hospital. If you are curious, ask who provides security at the hospital before you check in. If you have any special needs or concerns about your own personal security while at the hospital, let your doctor or nurse know and they can put you in touch with a security representative, probably through the patient services department.

COMPLAINTS

While hospital stays are rarely enjoyable, sometimes they are more uncomfortable than they have to be. If you have a complaint, whether it's about the food, the service, a member of the staff or anything else, there are several steps you can and should take while you are still in the hospital. First, bring your concern to the attention of the nurse or, if it is a staff problem, ask to speak to the supervising nurse or the charge nurse. If you do not get satisfaction after that or wish to pursue it further, you should ask to speak to someone from patient services (or the equivalent) and file a formal complaint. Many hospitals have an ombudsman who handles patient complaints. Most hospitals have complaint procedures that are spelled out in their patient handbook.

SMOKING

Given the politically-charged atmosphere that surrounds smoking today, it might be hard to believe that not too long ago both patients and visitors could smoke in certain sections of the hospital.

While researching this guide, I discovered numerous books and hospital guides published in the 1970s and '80s that advised patients checking into a hospital to request a "smoking room" if they liked to light up. Those days are history. I feel relatively comfortable in saying that there is probably not a single hospital in the nation today that allows patients or visitors to smoke *anywhere* inside the facility. It is possible that a "smoking room" might be provided for hospital staff members somewhere in the facility, but if you are a patient, plan on going cold turkey during your stay. If you are visiting, you'll probably be directed to an outside patio if you feel like having a cigarette.

It's also important to note that some hospitals will require patients who wish to smoke outside to first get permission from their doctor. If the hospital doesn't have the doctor's okay, you'll be asking for a stick of gum instead. Again, discuss this in advance with both your doctor and the hospital, before it leads to a misunderstanding.

CHECKING OUT

Your doctor will decide when you are ready to leave the hospital and he will likely tell you and/or your family at least a day before you are supposed to go home. You've probably seen the headlines and read the stories of patients being discharged before they were ready, but keep in mind your doctor and the hospital could be held liable if you are not medically stable at the time of discharge (unless you initiated it)—so it's extremely unlikely you will be sent home before you're ready.

In the event that you feel you have not recovered sufficiently, however, you should bring this to your doctor's attention immediately and candidly. Tell him why you feel you are not ready to go home. He will work with you and the hospital staff to see that your concerns are met, perhaps through a visiting nurse at home or some other alternative.

In some instances, patients decide to check out of a hospital on their own, against their doctor's and the hospital's advice. As long as you are determined to be lucid and of sound mind (i.e., not running a 107-degree fever and delirious), the hospital cannot force you to stay. They can and will, however, require you to sign a form that states you left the hospital against their advice and absolves them of any legal liability.

In most cases, your doctor will give you instructions regarding your care at home when he lets you know that you will be checking out. You'll be given directions on your medicine, activities to limit or take up and the date of your next appointment. Depending on the nature of your condition, a hospital social worker may also pay you a visit to help you with resources that will make your transfer back home go more smoothly. If you need professional homecare, the social worker can help. If you are concerned about some aspect of returning home, you can ask to see the social worker before you are discharged.

HOSPICE CARE

The core mission of a hospital is to help a person get better, to treat them and move them back home as soon as possible. For a person who is terminally ill, however, constantly doing the hospital shuffle—in and out and in and out—is a draining experience, one that often has little actual benefit.

A hospice is an alternative to hospitalization for the terminally ill who seek to live out their final days in a warm, loving and comfortable environment. At a hospice, the focus is on making the person as comfortable as possible during the final stages of their illness, *not* waging a medical last stand against the inevitable.

If you have questions about hospice care, ask to speak with a social worker at your hospital or ask your doctor.

The Emergency Room: Real Life Drama

"Medicine is the one place where all the
show is stripped of the human drama. You,
as doctors, will be in a position to see the
human race stark naked—not only physically,
but mentally and morally as well."

MARTIN H. FISCHER, FISCHERISMS

ER. It's hard to believe that two simple
letters could express so much. Chaos
and grace, loss and triumph...life and
death. Popular Hollywood dramas
aside, if you've been in one you know there

is little glamour to be found in a hospital's emergency room. For the patients (at least the ones who are conscious and lucid), the ER can be an understandably frightening experience, one that is filled with pain, panic, confusion and worse. For their loved ones in the waiting room, it's a grueling experience of waiting it out, one spent thumbing through magazines or trying to watch television in a room often filled with ER patients who haven't been admitted to the ward yet. Thus the lobby can be as lively (to put it nicely) as the unit, with coughing, moaning, vomiting and frustrated people pacing back and forth and asking the nurses "When is my wife going to be admitted? We've been here three hours!"

On the other side of those locked doors that separate the lobby from the actual ER, the picture isn't much prettier. It is here that the nitty-gritty battles for people's lives are fought every day. Car accidents, shooting victims, heart attacks, strokes…you name it, emergency rooms see it. Most of the time the staff of an ER can pull a patient back from the brink—at least for the moment. Other times, even their best efforts aren't enough. Death visits the ER perhaps more than any other unit in the hospital.

And perhaps it is precisely these high stakes that make the emergency room one of the most intriguing, and yet misunderstood, sections of the hospital. While planned hospitalizations continue to decline in many regions around the nation as a result of cost-cutting efforts and advances in outpatient therapies, in other areas (especially the major cities, where government continues cutting back services for the uninsured and underinsured) people are pouring into emergency rooms in record numbers. For many of us, a trip to the ER has been the only time we've been in a hospital.

Yet as Catherine Kaliel can attest, the vast majority of people entering an ER, either as patient or supporting family member, have little if any idea what an emergency room is for, how an ER functions, who works in it and who should be using it.

"Unfortunately, most people don't understand the basic nature of an ER and we see the result of that almost every day," says Kaliel, who is the director of emergency services at Citrus Valley Medical Center's Inter-Community campus, and the president-elect of the Emergency Nurses Association for Greater Los Angeles.

Kaliel reports that Inter-Community's 14-bed emergency room, which sees about 60 people a day, is repeatedly visited by people who shouldn't be there. Why? Quite simply because what they are using the ER for is not an emergency. It's a phenomenon that is repeated in ERs at many hospitals across the nation, particularly in the cities.

As Kaliel notes, this is a dangerous trend, as it swamps the unit and staff with cases that would otherwise be treated in a non-emergency setting, thus impacting care for those who truly need it.

WHAT IS AN ER?

Emergency rooms exist to treat people who are in danger of dying without immediate medical intervention. "Any condition a person has in which treatment delayed would result in loss of life or limb is an emergency room case," Kaliel says. Accordingly, emergency rooms are designed and staffed with one essential, short-term goal: saving the patient's life.

Many of the amenities that you would find in other hospital wings and units, from the pleasant decor to the television set, are nowhere to be found in an ER. While some ERs are designed with actual rooms, Kaliel says most are laid out in a standard ward fashion, with a group of gurneys spread around a nurses' station, which allows doctors and nurses constant visual contact with patients. When privacy is necessary, a curtain attached to a ceiling track (like the kind that can often be found in a standard two bed hospital room) can usually be pulled around a gurney.

WHO SHOULD BE USING AN ER (AND WHO SHOULDN'T BE...)

As stated earlier, emergency rooms are for people experiencing medical emergencies. It sounds simple, but the problem is that what appears to be an "emergency" to most people often doesn't meet the criteria established by qualified medical professionals. When your kid is running a fever of 102 in the middle of the night and is crying and vomiting, a trip to the local emergency room seems like a reasonable course of action. To be sure, if you are seriously in doubt about what's ailing your child or if you're concerned that lack of immediate medical diagnosis and treatment might endanger him—then erring on the side of caution is not only understandable but perhaps prudent.

Yet what Kaliel and thousands of other ER staffs confront every day and night are people seeking treatment for the flu, nausea, cuts, aches, pains and every other sort of low-grade medical condition you can imagine. Kaliel says flu season can wreak havoc on an ER, as children and the elderly pour in to be seen. Then there are the working parents who use the ER as an after-hours doctor's office or a 24-hour clinic. Most of these moms and dads can't get off work to take their child to the doctor (or more likely can't afford to take off work) and figure they can just tap into the ER when they get home. The uninsured and underinsured also figure heavily into ER populations, Kaliel says, as many of these people take advantage of the fact that aid in an ER will not be denied as a result of inability to pay. They essentially use the ER for free care.

If you are considering getting yourself or a family member to an ER, you should first determine if your situation is truly a medical emergency. One option, if time is not a factor, is to call your doctor's office (almost all doctors have 24-hour answering services that can page your doctor or the doctor who is on call). He'll be able to advise you on whether you need to go to the emergency room, and if he thinks you should, he might even meet you there.

HOW DOES AN ER FUNCTION?

Though often chaotic, the ER does operate according to a standard procedure that keeps this vital resource from disintegrating. It's important that you understand how an ER operates and what is expected of you while you are there, either in the waiting area or on a gurney. The more you know, the less frustrated you'll be.

Checking In

As Kaliel points out, there are basically two ways into an ER: walking in through the pedestrian entrance, or getting wheeled in through the ambulance/paramedic entrance.

If you walk into an emergency room, you will be greeted first by a triage nurse (usually an RN), whose job it is to determine the nature and severity of your illness or injury, and how soon you need to be seen. The triage nurse is going to question you about you or your loved one's medical problem and you should be prepared to provide them with as much information as possible. The nurse will classify your illness or injury into one of three categories: emergent, urgent or delayed. Emergent is the top priority, in which the situation must be dealt with at once (i.e., heart attack, major blood loss). Urgent means the situation is not life-threatening and does not have to be handled immediately. Delayed is the lowest priority in ER admissions, a classification that indicates the situation is not life-threatening at all (i.e., cut fingers, flu cases) and can wait. As frustrating as it may be for people walking into an emergency room, ERs rely upon this prioritizing in order to function smoothly.

If you are brought to the ER in an ambulance, you will usually receive immediate attention. This is because most people who find themselves in an ambulance really are suffering potentially life-threatening conditions. Emergency rooms

are often prepped and ready for these patients, as paramedics are in contact with the ER doctor via phone while they are at the scene and en route to the hospital.

This is important to remember, especially if you have been waiting in an ER lobby for several hours. The ambulance entrance is in a different location, so badly injured people are not rolled through a waiting room. As such, even if it might not seem that busy in the lobby, keep in mind that emergency cases are probably streaming into the unit.

Kaliel says that some people who frequently use ERs have caught on to the priority admission of ambulance patients and actually call paramedics when they think they need to go to the hospital, whether or not it's a life-threatening situation. These "regulars" who use an ambulance for a cab ride to the hospital are making a big mistake. Not only does it deny people who really need an ambulance or paramedics access to them, but they will be in for a rude awakening once they are rolled into the ER. As soon as a doctor or nurse determines through a screening exam that they, in fact, are not a medically emergent case, there is a good chance they will be placed in the waiting room with the walk-in patients. And they are still likely to get stuck with the bill for the ambulance ride. When it's all said and done, a non-emergency ambulance delivery to the ER can be an expensive cab ride for treatment that didn't come any faster than if you had walked in.

Paying for It

If you have been classified as having an urgent or delayed condition, you'll be waiting for at least a short period in the lobby. During this time you will talk with the registration staff member, who will ask you for your name, address, phone number, insurance policy information, date of birth, social security number, and such family information as the address and phone number of your nearest friend or relative. It's very important that you have as much as this information available as possible.

While emergency care is not denied on the basis of ability to pay, not having all of the necessary insurance information can leave you with a substantial bill. For example, if you are a member of an HMO, you might have to get approval for an ER visit that was not classified as a medical emergency by the ER doctors. If this permission is not granted, your insurance company might refer you to a nearby clinic they contract with, or have you see your primary care physician in the morning (again, only if it is not an emergency). If this happens, you can still be seen and treated at the ER, but you will be asked to sign a financial responsibility statement that obligates you to pay for the visit if your insurance company refuses to do so.

While emergency room bills are often exaggerated, they can be quite expensive. Just walking into an ER and undergoing an initial evaluation by the doctor will probably cost between $150 to $200. Additional treatment costs can pile up quickly. Lab work and X-rays can lead to an emergency room bill that runs into the thousands of dollars. The bill you receive as a result of your visit to the ER will most likely be an itemized invoice from a variety of sources, such as the emergency department group (which contracts its doctors out to the hospital—in essence this is the doctor's bill), the hospital (for using its facility), the lab (for any tests), and radiology (for any X-rays as well as the radiologist's fee for reading and interpreting the X-rays). Note: If a radiologist is not on duty when you are treated in an ER, the doctor treating you will read the X-ray, but the radiologist will read your X-ray the next day to confirm the doctor's analysis. This "quality control" process will result in a radiologist charge.

Common sense tells you to read the fine print when you sign any sort of contract or financial obligation statement and this is especially true for an emergency room visit. If you don't understand something, ask the registration staff member *before* you sign anything.

How Long will You be in the ER?

This depends on whether or not your condition requires you to be admitted to the hospital for additional care. If you are to be treated and sent home, you will probably be released within several hours, or as soon as you are stable enough to return home. If your doctor decides to have you admitted, you may be in the ER for several more hours, as your hospital room is assigned and prepared. There have been instances of patients spending as many as two days in an emergency room, waiting for a bed to open in the main hospital. Kaliel explains that while most hospitals have no shortage of beds, the nursing staff for each unit is based on the daily census, not the number of beds. During extremely busy times, such as flu season, it may be several hours or longer before a bed opens up in the hospital unit where you are to be transferred, though this is rare. If your stay in an ER is going to be fairly long, Kaliel says that the staff will try to have a proper hospital bed brought down for you, as the thinly-padded ER gurneys can become uncomfortable after awhile.

ER Visiting

Unlike other areas of the hospital, an ER is not designed to accommodate a steady flow of visitors and well-wishers to a patient's bedside, as such visits distract staff from the medical mission at hand. Accordingly, hospitals have very strict rules about access to the ER. Normally, no one is allowed back into an ER to see their loved one until the patient has been seen by a doctor and his condition has stabilized. Doctors and nurses can't treat a patient with emotional family members looking over their shoulders. Once a patient is stabilized, his family members are usually allowed back for short periods, one person at a time.

In cases of critical injury, where the patient is not expected to live, the family is usually moved out of the waiting room and into a nearby "grieving room." Here, they are kept informed of the patient's status and a priest or other spiritual counselor may be called. Social workers may also be brought in to help the family cope during the crisis. Getting moved into a grieving room doesn't mean the patient will not survive, it is merely a precaution meant to protect the family and ensure their privacy.

Security

As violent incidents in emergency rooms increase, many states have responded with legislation requiring hospitals to staff their ERs with security personnel. Some hospitals, such as Pomona Valley Hospital Medical Center, have security teams that employ canine units, similar to police dogs. While not always visible, security is never far away.

WHO WORKS IN AN ER?

Like other sections of the hospital, emergency rooms are staffed with a team of professionals—centered around physicians and nurses—who specialize in emergency care. The ER also taps into the other units of the hospital, such as radiology for X-rays or social services for psychological support and referrals, and is by no means an island unto itself.

Doctors

Physicians in an emergency room are most likely going to be board certified in emergency care. Board certification essentially means the doctor has been trained in this type of medicine and has passed a national exam to qualify. This was not always the case. Kaliel says that 20 years ago the emergency room was often staffed by doctors who were moonlighting from their regular practice. "You might have a plastic surgeon in there one night, a neurosurgeon working the next," she says. Of course, these were all licensed medical doctors, but there is little doubt that emergency medicine has come a long way; it is now a recognized specialty. If you are in an ER, it is probably too late to ask if the doctor is board certified in emergency care. Kaliel says in the few instances where the doctors are not certified, they probably have years of ER experience under their belts, so you are still likely to be in good hands. Hospitals will often use "contract" doctors to staff its emergency room, hiring them from physician groups that specialize in providing emergency care. Larger hospitals, such as university medical centers, are likely to have staff physicians in the ER.

Emergency room doctors do not have admitting privileges at the hospital. They treat and stabilize the patient, who is then referred back to the primary care physician.

Nurses

Like emergency room doctors, nurses in the ER are likely to be certified in emergency medicine. These nurses are known as Certified Emergency Nurses (CENs) and they are required to have experience in ERs and must pass a rigorous exam in order to be certified. Kaliel describes emergency room nurses as akin to a medical jack-of-all-trades. By necessity, their skills must be diverse enough to deal with whatever may walk or roll through those ER doors. They handle infants to the elderly and, as Kaliel puts it, "We have to know a lot about everything." But the goals of the ER nurse differ substantially from nursing staff throughout the rest of the hospital, in that their focus is on the short-term: stabilize the patient.

Support Staff

The ER doctors and nurses are often backed up by a variety of other staff members, depending on the size of the hospital. Larger hospitals are likely to have residents and interns working in the emergency room, while others have Emergency Medical Technicians (EMTs) that are certified by a county or national registry. EMTs are trained in basic first aid, such as wrapping extremities in bandages, applying splints, taking vital signs and more. They generally do not perform any invasive procedures, though they may draw blood. The ER is also likely to have its own secretarial staff to handle registration of the patients and other clerical duties.

CHAPTER

7

Social Services:
The Hospital's
Hidden Treasure

"'Tis not enough to help the feeble up,
but to support him after."

SHAKESPEARE, TIMON OF ATHENS

When people think of hospitals, they usually think of a clinical-looking building where medical treatments are delivered. A place where the gritty battles are waged to save lives, where babies are delivered, and where disease is defeated.

What most people don't know is that hospitals, as institutions, can be a critical resource for non-medical services for people facing a wide array of problems. Counseling, referrals and intervention on issues ranging from drug abuse to child neglect to coping with the loss of a loved one are all available at hospitals today.

When accessed by a patient or their family, a hospital's social services department can play a vital role in helping ease a person or family through a time of crisis. Social services are clearinghouses of information—and in health care, knowledge is certainly power.

THE SOCIAL WORKER

A hospital's front line foot soldier in the area of social services is the social worker. The state mandates that hospitals provide social services to patients, and social workers, who usually hold masters degrees, are experts at helping families deal with a wide range of medical and non-medical crises.

While most social workers are jacks-of-all-trades by necessity, larger hospitals are often staffed with social workers who specialize in specific areas or wings of the hospital. There may be a social worker who focuses on cancer patients in the oncology ward, while others may handle the maternity, pediatrics, or emergency room units.

Meagan Kramer is a social worker at Pomona Valley Hospital Medical Center in Pomona, California, a 100-year-old facility that has been ranked in the top 20 non-teaching hospitals in the nation (out of 296 such hospitals). One of six full-time social workers at the 437-bed facility, Kramer works in the emergency room, neurological-orthopedic and neonatal intensive care units of the hospital. Her job puts her in contact with almost every kind of social crisis imaginable. People suffering from AIDS, gunshot victims, suicide attempts, abused children, abused elderly people, rape victims....Kramer says she handles about eight patients a day, but usually has to juggle several cases at once.

Like a surgeon in a M*A*S*H unit, Kramer often finds herself running from case to case, struggling to help patients and families make it through grueling experiences. Yet, as she notes with a weary smile, "that's what we're here for."

How to Contact a Hospital Social Worker

In many cases the social worker will come to the patient or the patient's family first, which in fact is how most people discover that hospitals have social workers. Kramer says that doctors often request that a social worker drop by for a consultation with a patient or family. Nurses and other hospital staff who are in close contact with patients may also ask that a social worker contact a patient or a family who is going through a difficult time.

In certain situations—such as suspected child abuse, child neglect, elderly abuse or neglect, suicide attempts and rape cases—social workers are required to intervene. In such situations, the social worker wears many hats at once, offering much-needed help and referrals to victims and their families. They also act as a conduit for authorities, such as law enforcement agencies and county social services. Kramer says she also collects information from men and women believed to be responsible for abusing either their spouse or child or both, which can be a delicate process.

While social workers are often the first to make contact, Kramer is quick to point out that any time a patient or family would like to consult with a social worker, a meeting can usually be arranged quickly and easily. Patients or families can ask doctors, nurses, or hospital staff to make a referral to a social worker. If a patient or family doesn't feel comfortable asking their doctor or a treating nurse to make a referral, they can simply call the hospital and ask the switchboard to connect them directly with social services. Once connected with social services, the patient or family should ask to speak with a social worker and then explain their situation and needs.

One key thing that Kramer says patients and families need to remember is that social workers are not there to judge people, so patients and families who may be concerned about raising personal issues regarding drug use, sexuality or other problems need not worry. Such conversations are confidential and won't be shared without the patient's or family's permission. The only exceptions are cases of abuse or public health hazard, in which instance state law may require disclosure. In short, you can talk to the social worker about almost anything. These staff members are literally there with a sympathetic ear and can lend a helping hand.

What the Social Worker Can Do

One of the main functions of the hospital social worker is to help patients and families identify the specific help they need, locate where they can get it, and put them in contact with the source of the help. While identifying the help a patient or family needs might sound like an easy task, it can actually be quite a complex process, which is one of the reasons why patients and families often need a social worker's help.

Social workers not only address the immediate issue at hand (a suicide attempt, for example), but will also try to identify other corresponding problems the person or family is having that may have contributed to the crisis. It is often with these underlying problems that the social worker can be of the most help.

Because resources that provide families and patients with assistance are usually a patchwork of government agencies, support groups and private charities, actually tapping into the help that's available is usually far more difficult than just picking up the phone and dialing a number. Again, the social worker is there to help with accessing the help she has referred. She can even make the calls for a patient and family.

Below are some examples of the types of issues that social workers deal with regularly and a summary of what they can usually do to help.

Grief Counseling Few things can be more painful than losing a family member or a loved one. As Kramer notes, while doctors and nurses save many lives, and can even appear to be miracle workers at times, there is no escaping mortality. "There is lots and lots of death in hospital work and we help people deal with it," she says. This grief work is critical. Family and friends can experience a wide range of emotions in the days before and after a loved one dies. Guilt, anger, denial and overwhelming sadness can all take their toll on people. A social worker can help in a variety of ways.

When a patient is dying, social workers step in where

necessary to help the patient through the process. They can help them get their affairs in order, draft a durable power of attorney for health care, make dying patients and their family aware of tissue and organ donor programs (so that other lives might be saved) and, perhaps most importantly of all, a social worker can provide much-needed emotional support. Kramer says social workers will often accompany doctors into the room when a patient and/or their family is getting the news that the condition is terminal.

Depending on a physician's bedside manner, social workers may even act as something of an interpreter, translating medical jargon into easy-to-understand terms. Social workers also help ensure that families and friends have access to their loved one at the bedside (it's now standard hospital protocol to allow loved ones to gather around a dying patient's bedside). Immediately following a person's death, the social worker steps in as needed with an ear to listen and a shoulder to cry on. They can help families make funeral arrangements. If serious issues seem likely to persist among family members following a death, a social worker can recommend counseling for the family and make a referral to an appropriate therapist.

Substance Abuse Hospitals treat people who have drug and substance abuse problems every day. Sometimes this treatment occurs in the emergency room as a result of an overdose, other times the person may be getting treated for a related medical problem and hospital staff recognizes the symptoms of drug abuse. In either situation, a social worker is likely to be called upon to help. It's important for families to remember that social workers can't do much to help a person who doesn't want help. Yet for patients ready and willing to get clean and sober, the social worker can play a pivotal role in getting that monkey off their back.

The social worker will first try to identify the scope of the person's drug problem. Depending upon the nature of the patient's addiction, the social worker may make a referral to a sober living house, a detox program, or a maintenance program (such as a methadone clinic), as well as various support groups for both patient and family. The importance of such referrals can't be overstated. Many agencies that operate detox programs or clean living houses require a referral before a person is admitted. As the social

"Well, it's not quite the same, but it seems to be working!"

services that make up the so-called "safety net" of our society are overwhelmed with people needing help, a hospital's social worker can help patients and families determine what programs offer the best chance of success.

Child and Elderly Abuse/Neglect Unfortunately, one of the most common instances that hospital social workers are called in to deal with today are abused or neglected children. One of the darkest sides of this national tragedy are the newborns who are delivered drug-addicted. "Crack babies," for instance, are infants who became dependent on crack cocaine while in their mother's womb. Surprisingly, many parents aren't aware that states consider drug-addicted babies to be more than just a health concern, but in fact a serious violation of the law on the part of the parents. Of equal concern to the state are children who are suffering from neglect, and who often appear at hospitals malnourished and suffering from other symptoms of abandonment. A social worker is required by law to intervene in such cases.

In essence, the social worker becomes the baby or child's advocate. The social worker can take a variety of actions, depending on the situation. In cases where an infant is born drug-addicted, a mandatory child abuse report will be filed with the local department of Child Protective Services (CPS). This will also happen in cases where the baby is not born drug-addicted, but the mother's blood tests positive for drugs. If the situation is serious enough, based on the social worker's report, CPS can place a "hospital hold" on the infant, which prevents the parents from taking custody of their baby. In fact, drug-addicted babies usually require significant hospital care and will likely end up in the neonatal intensive care unit. A child suspected of suffering abuse or neglect will be referred to CPS for review, which can result in a hospital hold or removal of the child from the home.

Underscoring the widespread nature of the problem, social worker Kramer says she deals with drug-addicted babies and their parents at least several times a week, often times more. Besides acting as an advocate for the child, the social worker can also provide the parents and family with much needed help (see substance abuse section in this chapter). It is very important that families face the situation, understand the gravity of it and remain honest with the social worker. Parents who work with the social worker to provide what's best for their baby are far more likely to get their newborn back—and their own lives back on track— much sooner than those who don't.

While it happens less often, hospital social workers today are also called upon to help seniors who are victims of abuse and neglect. Many states now have laws that classify abuse and neglect of the elderly as specific crimes, which means that social workers will approach them in a manner similar to other cases of abuse, offering appropriate referrals, contacting authorities (such as Los Angeles County's Adult Protective Services, which operates in a similar fashion as Child Protective Services), and taking other steps to help the victim get out of an abusive situation.

Victims of Violent Crime Social workers can literally mean the difference between life and death for many victims of violent crime, especially in instances of domestic abuse. The social worker usually intercepts victims of violent crime where they are most often seen in hospitals: the emergency room. Here the social worker has to play a balancing act, since most victims of domestic violence attempt to cover up abuse, explaining away cuts, bruises and broken bones with stories about "falling down," "running into doors," or even "falling out of bed."

When abuse is suspected, the social worker will comfort the victim and try to discover the truth of what happened. This may also mean talking with the suspected abuser, who often accompanies the victim to the hospital. If domestic violence is suspected, the social worker is required by law to notify police, who will make contact with the victim at the hospital.

While it's difficult to deal with, a victim of domestic abuse and their family members must understand that a social worker can help the most when the victim wants to make a change in their life. A social worker can make an immediate referral to a battered woman's shelter, can advise where and how to get a restraining order from the court, can make counseling referrals for both the abused and the abuser and much more. The social worker can provide the same help for victims of other violent crimes, such as rape and sexual assault. Counseling can be crucial for a person who has been violated and the social worker can get the victim the help they need.

Suicide Attempts/Mental Health When a person has tried to take their own life, they are usually taken to an emergency room, where a social worker will make an initial evaluation of the patient. Kramer points out that at Pomona Valley Hospital Medical Center, a social worker can call in a crisis team from the nearby Tri-City Mental Health Center. The crisis team can make a legal declaration of "5150" (the Welfare and Institution Code section for someone who is mentally disturbed) and take the patient into custody for a 72-hour evaluation. With court approval, a patient's evaluation and treatment can be extended by a matter of weeks. The social worker can help families cope with a loved one who is suffering from a mental disorder or who has attempted suicide by making referrals to appropriate programs.

Support Groups Most hospital social workers have resource directories and program guides the size of phone books, which enable them to steer a patient or a family to the program or service that best suits their needs. Social workers also often coordinate their *own* support groups at the hospital where they work. Pomona Valley Hospital Medical Center, for example, offers a variety of support groups that are coordinated by its social workers, including a perinatal loss group (for parents and families who have lost children at or near birth), several cancer patient groups and a caregiver's support group. Hospitals often offer a wide array of such programs, so it's best that patients and family members ask their hospital's social worker what groups are available. If a particular program is not available at one hospital, it may be available at another one nearby and can be accessed through a referral.

What Hospital Social Workers Don't Do!

While their responsibilities are many, hospital social workers do not handle welfare applications, food stamp applications or social security requests. This may seem obvious, but Kramer reports that patients and families mistakenly believe hospital social workers can process or expedite such applications. They cannot.

The Maternity Unit: Where Babies Come From

"To my embarrassment I was
born in bed with a lady."

WILSON MIZNER

Congratulations! You're having a baby.
Chances are you got the news from
a home pregnancy test and then had it
confirmed by your family doctor, but
questions are still swirling through your
happy head: what now? You've got a lot of
hopes—technology has never been better for the delivery of
babies. You've got more than a few fears—new mothers are

being cycled out of the recovery rooms in record speeds (a practice known as "drive-thru" deliveries). You've heard a lot, but you don't know much.

The decisions you make immediately following a positive pregnancy test result are very important, so it's vital that you know the options available to you and your family.

The good news is that in today's American health care system, a baby is a commodity. Hospitals know that you can choose to have your baby pretty much anywhere you want—including your own home—so competition for your business can be fierce.

SHOPPING FOR DOCTORS AND HOSPITALS

Chelly Coon, director of the Maternal/Child Health units at Citrus Valley Medical Center's Inter-Community and Queen of the Valley campuses in Southern California, notes that pregnant women and their husbands today need to literally shop around for the hospital and doctor that will deliver their baby. Medical insurance will play an important role in determining where a family can have their baby delivered, but Coon says that having insurance doesn't necessarily mean a family can't shop around. Insurance companies today, particularly in the managed care markets in the West, generally operate a pool of hospitals, clinics and medical groups which can be tapped by their subscribers.

Families may also consider alternative birthing practices, such as having the baby at home with the assistance of a mid-wife or a nurse practitioner. Another option available to families are birth centers. Coon reports that these types of deliveries are becoming more common for low-risk pregnancies, which are the vast majority of pregnancies in the U.S. today.

Once an expecting family determines they will be using a hospital and an obstetrician to deliver their baby, they need not be shy or beat around the bush as they hunt for the physician and institution. These are literally job interviews and, in most cases, the family should realize that they are in the driver's seat.

Most hospitals maintain a continually updated directory of physicians. This can be a good resource if you are searching for an obstetrician. Just call the hospital maternity unit's nursing station and ask for a referral.

But as Coon notes, it is imperative that families, and particularly the expectant mother, sit down and talk with any prospective obstetrician. At issue should be the doctor's experience, preferences in delivery rooms and style of delivery. Doctors usually build up a word-of-mouth clientele, but you should ask for several references—other families for whom the doctor has delivered babies—and follow up on them. A good bedside manner is important, but a warm personality doesn't always translate into an excellent skill level. A balance has to be sought and the mother and family should be looking for that balance during the interviews with doctors.

Ultimately, Coon says, women need to feel good about their selection of an obstetrician and should be looking for someone they "click" with. Many expecting mothers today

Delivery Choices

feel more comfortable working with a female doctor and Coon says these moms shouldn't hesitate to voice that preference, especially when seeking a referral.

Just as doctors should be interviewed before being selected to deliver a baby, families should also take a close look at the hospital they'll be using. Many hospitals actually give tours of the maternity unit, allowing mothers and fathers to check out everything from the decor to the staff. During these tours, prospective patients/customers are usually encouraged to ask plenty of questions of the staff. This is a great time to find out what sort of pre-birth assistance the hospital offers, how busy the maternity unit usually is (this can impact whether the mother is sharing a room with another mother during labor), what sort of neonatal intensive care unit they have (in the event of complications at birth), what security measures the maternity unit employs, how fast mothers are usually sent home and what sort of follow-up care the hospital offers.

While you are shopping for a hospital in your area, call around and find out which ones have tours of the maternity unit. If a particular hospital doesn't have an actual tour of the unit, ask their community relations staff or some of the maternity unit's nursing staff if it would be all right for you to come down and take a look around. This shouldn't be a problem as long as it's scheduled in advance. Don't just drop in on them and start poking around the unit.

WHAT TO LOOK FOR AND ISSUES TO CONSIDER

Obviously a lot has changed since the days when an expectant father paced the floor of the waiting room, fresh cigars in his coat pocket, waiting for any word of whether it's a boy or a girl. Perhaps more than at any time since the frontier days—when families *had* to be involved in childbirth—relatives have more access to America's delivery rooms.

Yet just how much freedom you and your family may enjoy during the delivery of your child needs to be discussed and established up front. As Coon notes, a doctor's bedside manner is often a good indicator of what type of birthing experience the family can expect from that physician. A doctor that is more cold and clinical is probably going to be less likely to allow the family—or even the mother—much control over how the baby is delivered. The more open the physician, the more likely the family will be able to wield more control in the birth of their baby.

DADS, SIBLINGS AND
VIDEO CAMERAS

In some instances today, fathers are allowed, and even encouraged by the doctor, to participate in the actual birthing process. Fathers no longer have to be relegated to a distant room filled with their nervous buddies—unless of course they want to be. Dads are usually allowed in the delivery room now and sometimes siblings are too, though hospitals often have age requirements for other children to be in the room.

As with every other aspect of our society, video cameras are also often allowed in the delivery room so that families can capture the moment. But again, as Coon notes, it all depends on what the doctor says. There are still many doctors today who are traditionalists, and they don't like the idea of a dad peering over their shoulder as they work, or having a video camera capturing their every move.

To be fair, this issue doesn't always boil down to whether or not the physician is "progressive" or "old-fashioned." Coon notes that there are legal issues that doctors have to consider. At Citrus Valley's Inter-Community campus, for example, families are usually allowed to video a birth during the labor and then just moments after the delivery when the baby is placed on the warming table. The hospital requires video cameras be turned off as the baby's head emerges from the womb and won't allow them turned back on until the baby has been completely delivered. The hospital's policy is based on protecting the doctor from a litigation concern should complications arise during the delivery, Coon says.

Aside from video, some doctors today don't mind if dads-to-be take a literal "hands-on" role in the delivery of their child. One doctor at Inter-Community will allow a father to actually deliver his baby while the doctor stands at his side, ready to intervene if necessary. Fathers are also allowed to cut and tie the umbilical cord.

Another important aspect to consider is visitation hours. Many hospitals today allow the spouse or partner 24-hour visitation with the mother, meaning that he gets to spend the night in the room with her if he wishes.

Again, if family members would like to play an active role in the entire birthing process, it is important that those desires are established very early on with the doctor and hospital so there are no misunderstandings when the moment arrives.

SECURITY SYSTEMS

Another crucial element to consider when inspecting a maternity unit is the infant security system. Families need to be aware that infant abductions from hospitals do happen and some states require hospitals to have security systems in place wherever infants are cared for. Hospital staff should be able to answer any questions about security precautions in the maternity unit.

DELIVERY ROOMS:
TRADITIONAL VS. LDRS

Just as families need to interview doctors about who will play a role in the birthing process, they also need to determine just what kind of delivery room the doctor prefers to use. Most doctors generally use one hospital or a group of hospitals, so it's important to make sure the doctor has access to the type of maternity unit that your family desires.

Traditional delivery rooms still exist, but these throwbacks to the 1960s are generally cold and sterile in appearance. This clinical environment can come as something of a shock to a new mother who has just been wheeled in from the comfortable surroundings of the labor room, which is usually very homey and warm. Flowery wallpaper, billowy curtains and soft lights are suddenly replaced with tiled walls, stainless steel fixtures and spotlights more fitting for a police interrogation than a baby's birthday.

In an effort to appeal to today's sensibilities, many hospitals have combined the three or four traditional stages of the birthing process into one single room, known as LDRs or LDRPs, for Labor-Delivery-Recovery or Labor-Delivery-Recovery-Postpartum.

These multi-purpose rooms generally appear more like a bedroom than a high-tech delivery room, yet that's exactly what they are. These LDRs also help keep the mother and family from being shunted about from one room to another before, during and after her labor. Coon says keeping the

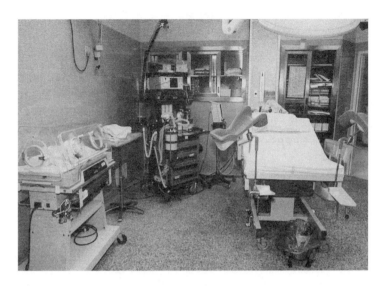

Traditional delivery room

Photos by Walt Weis

LDR, Labor-Delivery-Recovery

process as centralized as possible is generally better, as it helps the family and staff to remain focused.

Coon points out that many doctors either prefer or don't mind using state-of-the-art LDRs or LDRPs, but adds that there are some doctors who refuse to use anything but a traditional delivery room, which is why a family needs to find these things out early on.

PRE-BIRTH CLASSES AND LAMAZE

While Lamaze is typically associated with the breathing techniques that help the delivery of the baby go more smoothly, Lamaze is actually a series of pre-birth classes that offer mothers—and their supporters, be it fathers or friends—a host of information to help them through childbirth.

More than 150,000 Lamaze classes are taught in the United States every year and are attended by well over 2 million parents.

The practice and philosophy of Lamaze was established by Dr. Ferdinand Lamaze, a doctor who introduced his native France to birthing techniques originally developed by the Russians. In the 1950s, the technique became popularized in the United States when a woman wrote an article that described her birthing experience using Lamaze.

As an overall approach to childbirth, Lamaze classes stress that giving birth is a collective effort and experience, and they encourage mothers to include and share the responsibility with her mate or another person of her choosing.

Women attending these pre-birth classes will learn about birthing options, pain management skills (including relaxation, support and breathing techniques), and strategies to promote a vaginal delivery in order to reduce the risk of having a Caesarean section. Advocates of Lamaze note the impact the philosophy has had on the American health care system by pointing to the development of home-like LDRs, the appearance of fathers in the delivery room, and the advent of sibling and family involvement.

Doctors will generally refer a mother to a Lamaze class as her pregnancy progresses. Hospitals or birth centers, where the classes are usually held, can provide more information on what classes are available.

While Lamaze techniques can also be learned through other sources, such as books or videos, advocates note that attending the actual classes is important because it allows the mother to voice questions or concerns to childbirth instructors.

The American Society for Psychoprophylaxis in Obstetrics (ASPO), a non-profit Lamaze advocacy group, suggests mothers and their partners consider several different factors when looking for a childbirth preparation class.

The qualifications of the childbirth educator are critical. The instructor should be certified by a nationally recognized organization, such as ASPO. Class size is also an important factor. ASPO recommends that classes be kept to between 8 to 12 couples. You don't want to learn Lamaze while packed into a room like a sardine. The class should also have a focus that reaches beyond basic information about pregnancy and childbirth. Instructors should discuss birthing options in general and then be able to help couples develop their own individualized birth plan.

If you select to have your baby in a hospital, Coon suggests attending the Lamaze classes at that hospital, as maternity unit staff members often take part in the classes and it's a good way to get to know the staff and see how they operate.

AFTER DELIVERY

Once your baby has been delivered, barring complications, chances are you'll be going home within a day. Most hospitals release non-complicated vaginal deliveries after 24 hours. While that time span may seem quite short following such a physically and emotionally draining experience, it is substantially longer than the so-called "drive-thru" deliveries, in which mothers were cycled out of the hospital in as little as six hours after delivery. Federal law now requires hospitals keep a mother 24 hours after the birth. Caesarean section deliveries generally result in the mother staying in the hospital for 48 hours or longer. Still, it is important to ask about the standard discharge policy when you are selecting a hospital.

If there were complications during the delivery or if the baby was born sick, the hospital may discharge the mother but keep the baby, usually in a neonatal intensive care unit (NICU). Most hospitals that have NICUs allow parents to remain with the baby in the unit, if they desire. These units, however, are not typical hospital rooms with beds and televisions and chairs. They are packed with hi-tech medical equipment and look more like a space-age nursery.

Once they discharge a new mother, many hospitals will send a visiting nurse over to the family's home the following day as a courtesy call to make sure everything is going well. The nurse will check the baby for jaundice, which is common in newborns, and make sure the umbilical cord—where the belly button now exists—is healing properly. The nurse can also help the mother with any feeding problems she may be having, which is critical in the days immediately following birth.

The Oncology Unit: Battling the "Big C"

"While there are several chronic diseases more destructive than cancer, none is more feared."

DR. CHARLES H. MAYO

The C-word.

When a doctor utters the word "cancer," it can land a punch that often staggers the patient. The word is so psychologically stunning that some doctors shy away from using it all when talking with a patient who has just been diagnosed with a form of the disease.

"It's absolutely devastating to hear you've been diagnosed with cancer. The scare is still here," says Jill McCormick, assistant director of oncology at Citrus Valley Medical Center's Queen of the Valley campus. "When most people hear the word 'cancer,' they immediately have visions of someone they knew with cancer or what they've heard happens to you when you have cancer, which is: you get very sick, are treated with things that make you sicker, your hair falls out, you are in constant pain and then you die."

Not a pretty picture, is it?

A DEADLY DISEASE, BUT NO LONGER A DEATH SENTENCE

To say that cancer is no longer a devastating, deadly disease that wreaks havoc on the lives of those who have it as well as their loved ones would be false, but there is no question that if you find yourself heading into an oncology unit in America today, much has changed for the better.

Treatments have become more refined and more effective as medical science has closed in on the disease. New medicines are now available that will help you become less sick, or not sick at all, following the traditional treatments of chemotherapy and radiation.

Perhaps just as important as the medical advances against cancer are the social support systems that have sprouted up across the nation. If you are diagnosed with cancer today, you will be able to plug into a network of patient advocacy groups, caregiver support groups and cancer information centers that will keep you informed about the most recent medical advances and cutting edge treatments. The bottom line is that modern Western medicine has progressed considerably in its war on cancer.

ONCOLOGY: A FULL-SERVICE UNIT

Cancer units in hospitals today (usually known as oncology units) treat almost every known type of cancer, with the 12 major forms of the disease being prostate cancer, breast cancer, lung cancer, colorectal cancer, bladder cancer, non-Hodgkin's lymphoma, uterine cancer, melanoma, kidney cancer, leukemia, ovarian cancer and pancreatic cancer.

Skin cancer is perhaps the most common cancer of all, but with the exception of the deadly melanoma, it is usually treated on an outpatient basis through a dermatologist's office.

The size and scope of a hospital's oncology unit will vary, with some bigger hospitals (such as teaching hospitals) specializing in the treatment of cancer and offering access to new technology and experimental drug treatments (usually known as "investigational therapies").

Mid-size and smaller hospitals will probably combine their cancer unit with another ward, which can be more economical. McCormick notes that at the Queen of the Valley campus, the 44-bed oncology unit handles the overflow from the medical surgery unit and sees a host of different kinds of patients, including people with AIDS (who often are diagnosed with various cancers, some of them rare, such as Karposi Sarcoma), lung disease patients, people with kidney failure and heart disease. Cancer is the primary focus of the unit, however.

WHAT THE ONCOLOGY UNIT DOES

There are basically two types of patients coming into an oncology unit: those who have already been diagnosed with cancer and are being treated for the disease, and those who have not yet been diagnosed, but are undergoing tests to determine if they have the disease.

McCormick says most of the patients and families she sees in her unit know very little if anything about the disease or how a cancer unit functions at a hospital. "A lot of them are really in the dark and frightened," she says. "We'll get family members in here saying 'My dad has cancer, what's he doing in the *oncology* unit?!"

Accordingly, one of the priorities of the staff is to educate incoming patients and their families about what to expect during the course of their treatments, to dispel confusing myths, and to explain new developments in treatment.

A cancer unit is very similar to other hospital units in some regards and quite different in others. Depending on the hospital, an oncology unit may be equipped to handle both adult and pediatric cases, though they are often separated. Pediatric oncology is a subspecialty that some hospitals don't handle. In such cases, the patient may be referred to a children's hospital.

The patient rooms in an oncology unit are not much different than other sections of the hospital, though cancer units sometimes have more flexible visiting hours and allow family members (one at a time) to spend the night in the room. At Queen of the Valley, for example, a sleeping chair can be placed next to the bed for a family member who wants to spend the night with their loved one.

Another noticeable difference in the oncology unit is the close rapport between the nursing staff and their patients. The chronic nature of the disease results in repeated and prolonged stays for the patients, and through the years the hospital staff naturally develops strong personal relationships with them. "We see a lot of regulars in here," McCormick says. Those relationships can become as important as the treatment itself.

TREATMENTS

While new therapies and treatments are being developed (such as photodynamic or laser therapy), there are still three primary forms of cancer treatments delivered through oncology units: radiation, chemotherapy and surgery. Depending on the type of cancer and its stage of development, the oncologist may call for any one or a combination of all three treatments to battle the disease.

These treatments are very complex, which is one of the reasons why people with cancer often have a difficult time understanding how their doctors are fighting the disease that is ravaging their body. For example, the following is a description of the Division of Radiation Oncology at USC/Kenneth Norris Jr. Comprehensive Cancer Center:

Battling the "Big C"

"The USC Department of Radiation Oncology is one of the few full-service facilities in the United States, with its multi-leaf collimator (MLC) equipped linear accelerator, CT-based radiotherapy simulator, high dose-rate afterloading brachytherapy and clinical hypertherapy."

The standard health care consumer has about as much chance understanding that description as he does a targeting guidance system on an ICBM.

If your doctor hasn't explained how the treatments he has prescribed work, ask him to do so in a manner you can understand. The nurses in a cancer unit will also fill you in about how the treatment you are scheduled to undergo works, as well as what side effects you can expect in the aftermath.

Radiation

This involves targeting cancer with radioactive isotopes, which can kill or shrink tumors or delay the spread or growth of a cancer. There can be many side-effects, including loss of hair, weight loss, dry or blotchy skin and more. Many hospitals now contract out radiology services, so you may receive this treatment on an outpatient basis at a radiology center or, if you are an inpatient, be transferred there for treatment. For example, Queen of the Valley uses a radiology center that is right next door to the hospital.

Chemotherapy

This is basically a potent cocktail of medicine, administered through an IV, that kills the cancer cells in your body. Unfortunately, it kills the "good" cells as well, which can lead to a host of side effects, such as nausea, hair loss, weight loss and more. Hospitalization can be required during chemotherapy, especially in leukemia patients undergoing "induction chemotherapy"—a process that wipes out the blood cell count completely.

Other types of chemotherapy can be administered on an outpatient basis, or can be delivered through the hospital's oncology unit, depending on the dosage your oncologist has requested. For a short-stay treatment, you may check into an oncology unit in the morning for the "prep work," which includes IVs so you don't dehydrate and medicine to limit the side effect of nausea, before the actual chemotherapy begins. You may be in the unit for several hours after the treatment has been administered for observation and then be released by that evening.

If your doctor has prescribed a more intense program of chemotherapy, you may find yourself in the cancer unit for several days, during which time the treatment will be administered in 24-hour cycles.

Chemotherapy can be used as either a maintenance program to keep the cancer from spreading or as a "cure," where the goal is to wipe out the cancer completely (when possible). It is also used by doctors as a treatment to decrease the pain cancer patients sometimes experience.

If you are undergoing chemotherapy you will probably be returning to the hospital's cancer unit on a regularly scheduled basis for treatments, such as every four to six weeks.

Surgery

Sometimes doctors may decide the best way to attack the cancer is to literally go in and remove it from the body. This is especially true for tumors or precancerous tissues which are at a high risk for turning cancerous. Surgery is often conducted in conjunction with other treatments, such as radiation. If you are to undergo surgery for cancer, you will be prepped in an oncology unit and placed there after the surgery (or possibly the ICU) for observation.

RESOURCES

Most oncology units offer help far beyond traditional medical treatments for cancer patients. As McCormick notes, the cancer unit at Queen of the Valley introduces patients and families to an assortment of resources that can help them cope with the disease.

Nurses educate patients and their families in the use of feeding tubes (also known as G-tubes), IVs and the administering of medications. This is especially important in the face of shorter hospital stays and a growing emphasis on outpatient and home care.

Additional services the unit offers includes breast prosthesis programs and clothing classes (for mastectomy patients), low cost and free wig programs, sexuality courses that deal with impotence (a common side effect from prostate cancer surgery) and a variety of social support groups for both patients and caregivers.

Remember that you are probably going to be in for the long haul when considering treatment for cancer at a hospital (leukemia patients can find themselves in a cancer unit for up to six weeks at a time), so the scope and depth of the services they offer aside from the specific medical treatment is very important.

Find out in advance what sort of support services they offer. Ask for patient or family references, someone you can talk with who has been treated through the unit. Ask if the unit is involved in any clinical trials for new cancer treatments for which you may be a candidate. Breast cancer patients at Queen of the Valley, for example, recently participated in trials for the new drug Taxol.

If you are selecting an oncologist, find out how long he has specialized in this form of medicine and what, if any, sub-specialties he may have. Again, ask for references.

▶ Does the hospital you are considering have a dedicated oncology unit with specialized staff?

▶ Does the unit's nursing staff have special training in oncology and chemotherapy administration? At Queen of the Valley Hospital, for example, nurses in the oncology unit are specially trained in the administration of chemotherapy.

▶ Does the hospital offer a multidisciplinary approach to the care of oncology patients? Do they offer an approach that combines social services, dietary support, pharmacy support, physical therapy, pastoral care and discharge planning support? This "big picture" approach will be better for you as a patient.

▶ Does your treating physician specialize in oncology? It is possible for doctors who are not oncologists to treat cancer patients at hospitals where they have admitting privileges. If you have any doubt, ask.

▶ Does the hospital offer cancer support groups and resources?

▶ Is the hospital accredited by the Commission on Cancer? This national organization sets standards and checks the quality of participating hospitals' oncology units.

The Oncology Unit

▶ Does the hospital offer a full range of treatment options? Chemotherapy, radiation, surgery and palliative care should all be options at your disposal if needed and appropriate for your illness.

▶ Does the hospital offer ongoing tumor boards or cancer conferences for the unit's physicians, nurses and ancillary staff? This is important, as it allows the treating staff to discuss and establish team approaches to a patient's illness. This is how ideas get fleshed out among the staff.

▶ Does your hospital encourage family participation and have flexible visiting hours for oncology patients?

The Cardiology Unit: Have a Heart

"The most important thing in illness is never to lose heart."

NIKOLAI LENIN

 From English doctor William Harvey's first description of the process of blood circulation in the early 1600s to the first open heart surgery of the 1930s to the first artificial heart transplant of the 1980s, the medicine of the human heart has traveled a long and complex road.

In America, however, the medical advances in cardiology have been countered by a rise in the incidence of heart disease. Prior to the Industrial Revolution, heart disease was not a major killer. Today, it kills more people in the United

States than any other illness. Two of every five Americans will die of cardiovascular disease, with more than 2,500 dying from it every day. As many as 50 million Americans suffer from high blood pressure, one of the leading causes of heart disease, yet as many as one-third of those people aren't even aware of their condition.

Accordingly, cardiology units play a major role in hospitals, from both an educational as well as treatment standpoint. Some hospitals feature "heart care" centers, complete with a staff of surgeons, doctors and nurses that specialize in heart disease and disorders.

Pam Karns is the director of the cardiovascular and critical care services program at Citrus Valley Medical Center's Inter-Community campus, which combines an array of units into its overall cardio program.

Under the cardio umbrella falls surgical ICU, coronary unit, cardiac cath lab, ambulatory care (an outpatient service), cardiology department and the cardiovascular data department. As hospitals continue to experiment with what's known in the health care industry as "reengineering"— essentially new configurations of administration and departments—more hospitals are combining units like those at Inter-Community.

WHAT HAPPENS IN THE CARDIOLOGY UNIT?

How you end up in a hospital's cardiology unit and what happens to you once you get there will depend upon your specific symptoms and condition. Once your primary care doctor has referred you to a cardiologist (as a result of chest pains, for example), the cardiologist will do a general work-up on you.

Karns says you will likely be asked a lot of questions, such as:

▸ What kind of pain are you having?

▸ How frequently?

▸ What are your activity levels at those times?

▸ What is the quality of the pain?

▸ When does the pain occur?

▸ Are you having difficulty breathing?

"The cardiologist will be looking for clues from the patient," Karns says. She notes there are a lot of different kinds of chest pain that people come to the hospital with that aren't heart problems. Stomach pain, for example, can feel a lot like chest pain. In certain disorders, chest pain can be caused during inhaling and exhaling, unrelated to the heart. "A lot of what we do initially is rule other possibilities out," Karns states.

The specialist may also order a non-invasive process, such as an echo cardiogram (sort of a sonogram of the heart, allowing doctors to detect abnormalities), an EKG (basically a photo of your heart, giving the doctor a variety of views) or a stress test.

Standard blood tests may also be administered, including those that will look at your cholesterol, lipid and oxygen saturation levels.

You may also undergo an invasive test in a cath lab, where a catheter is threaded into your body, allowing doctors to look at your heart and check for blockages or other problems. A decision could be made at that time whether surgery is needed or not.

If you need surgery on a non-emergency basis, you will meet with the cardiac surgeon before the operation for a debriefing. If you are strong enough, you may get a tour of the cardio ICU unit. If not, you will probably get a verbal walk-through of the process and the various units involved.

The staff will provide you with pre-operation education as well as an explanation of what to expect following the

"Yes, Igor I like chocolates, but it's still the wrong heart!"

surgery. "Essentially we are providing the patient with a 'care map,' something that guides them through the process," Karns says. "We teach them what they need to be prepared to do. Things like breathing deep, even if it hurts. We prepare them for the possibility of coming out of surgery on a ventilator. They need to be ready for the possibility that they will wake up with a tube in their throat."

Other pre-surgery prep work is likely to include an EKG, a chest X-ray and more blood tests. Also, if you are undergoing scheduled surgery, you may be offered the opportunity to donate your own blood in advance of the operation. This blood may be used during the procedure and afterwards if additional transfusions are needed.

POST-CARDIO CARE

You will remain in the surgical intensive care unit for observation and care after surgery. During this time, rest is extremely important, and as a result there may be greater restrictions on visitors, activities and anything else that may inhibit your recovery or put stress on your heart. Karns says inpatient stays range from three to six days but can be as high as eleven days in the hospital.

Patient education is as vital in a cardiac unit as in other wings of the hospital. Multiple health care team members will teach you and your family about heart health, providing information on everything from diet and exercise to support groups for heart disease patients and their caregivers.

LIFESTYLE CHANGES

Your cardiologist and nursing staff will spell out the limitations that you will likely be facing once you are discharged.

Some of the lifestyle changes you may encounter during your recovery are:

▶ You may be put on a moderate exercise program.

▶ You may be advised not to drive.

▶ You may have to abstain from sex or heavy physical exertion for awhile.

▶ You may have to alter your diet, including cutting out sodium (salt).

Staff will also advise you on the medications that you'll be taking at home, informing you about what each one does and when to take them. Depending on your situation, a home health nurse may be assigned to you. In such instances, a nurse will come to your house to check up and help coordinate your care.

QUESTIONS TO ASK AND THINGS TO CONSIDER

▶ When considering heart surgery, you should ask your doctor about the credentials of the institution, the staff and the attending doctor or surgeon with whom you will be working.

▸ What is the surgeon's level of experience?

▸ Look for a hospital with a high success ratio. Ask the hospital and the physician for their national mortality score. The surgeon may be reluctant to tell you, but the hospital should willingly disclose their ratio.

▸ You want a cardiologist who will be straightforward with you. Look for one who will give you an easy-to-understand evaluation, who will break down the potential outcomes of medical management, who will list your surgery options along with their risk factors (surgeons should be able to break it down to a numeric percentage, i.e., "the surgery has an 85% chance of success." But remember, these are ball-park numbers).

▸ Find out what limitations you are going to be facing following surgery and/or treatment and how much educational support the hospital's cardiology unit will be able to provide you and your family.

▸ As always, ask your doctor about alternatives to the suggested treatment, though with heart bypass surgery there may not be many viable choices.

CHAPTER

11

The Pulmonary Unit: Breathing Lessons

"Welcome, sulfur dioxide
hello, carbon monoxide
the air, the air is everywhere
breath deep, while you sleep
breath deep...."

FROM THE MUSICAL HAIR

 We rarely think about the daily function and health of our lungs until we have a problem breathing—and then we tend to panic.

If you're from the city, those two weeks in the countryside or down at the beach seem to do wonders for your airways, don't they? If you're a smoker, you can feel the difference in your chest after quitting for just one day.

The fact is that for millions of Americans the idea of "breathing easy" is like an elusive dream. These people aren't waiting to exhale, they're doing their best just to inhale. For those who suffer from Chronic Obstructive Pulmonary Disease (COPD) or "lung disease"—which affects as many as 25 million Americans— breathing is an everyday struggle. Each climb up a stairway or walk down a hallway leaves them feeling like they just ran the hundred yard dash. Gasping for air is a daily experience.

According to Dr. Brian Tiep, hospitals began to develop comprehensive pulmonary programs about 30 years ago while treating people suffering from COPD. Dr. Tiep co-created the pulmonary program at the City of Hope in Southern California during the early 1970s, and is now designing the new pulmonary program at Pomona Valley Hospital Medical Center.

BIG NEED, SHORT SUPPLY

Despite a substantial need for such programs, comprehensive pulmonary programs are in short supply around the nation. Tiep estimates that about one in every three hospitals has such a program, which translates to approximately 10,000 slots available to treat patients on both an inpatient and outpatient basis. That means less than one-tenth of one percent of people who need comprehensive pulmonary rehabilitation in America actually have access to it. The good news is that pulmonary programs educate and train people how to manage their lung disease, giving them the tools to institute their own program at home.

Accordingly, Tiep says it is vital for people who have lung disease—especially if they are in the early stages of it—to educate themselves about the condition, talk with their doctor and locate the programs available in their area. Even if it means traveling a reasonable distance to access a program, it is important to get involved as soon as possible. The earlier you get a jump on COPD, the better.

WHAT IS LUNG DISEASE?

Lung disease is the term often used to describe a variety of conditions which impact a person's breathing, such as asthma, chronic bronchitis, emphysema and pulmonary fibrosis. Because symptoms from these conditions often appear at the same time, physicians refer to them under the umbrella term Chronic Obstructive Pulmonary Disease (or sometimes as Chronic Obstructive Lung Disease—COLD).

Your lungs collect oxygen from the air that is sucked in through the nose and mouth and release carbon dioxide waste every time you exhale. Your lungs are made up of airways and about 700 million air sacs. Lung disease, in its various forms, is a progressive breakdown of your body's ability to process the air you breathe, usually because your airways are becoming constricted or the air sacs are being destroyed.

Lung disease can develop unchecked in a person for years, and even decades, before it is diagnosed. As the average healthy person has 10-times the amount of lung capacity needed for restful, easy breathing, most people will lose much of that capacity before the symptoms become apparent. Tiep says there is a "tip of the iceberg" phenomenon with lung disease, in that those who have been diagnosed only represent a fraction of those who actually have the disease.

It should be no surprise that smoking is the leading cause of lung disease (as well as causing a host of cancers and other health conditions that kill half a million Americans every year). Tiep estimates that 90% of emphysema cases are directly related to smoking.

The following are four specific conditions that fall under the term lung disease:

Asthma Asthma is caused by the choking off of the airways through swelling tissue and the build-up of mucous. People with asthma often suffer "attacks," characterized by coughing, weezing and labored breathing. These episodes can be triggered by a number of things, such as allergies, dust, over-exercising or even laughing or crying. Asthma is a condition that, with proper management, can go into long periods of remission.

Bronchitis This condition is caused by the swelling of the lining in the airways. It is marked by extreme coughing and copious mucous production.

Emphysema Emphysema occurs when the lung tissue is destroyed. The lungs' air sacs—which gather oxygen—become so stretched out they can no longer do the job.

Pulmonary Fibrosis This condition is caused by scar tissue building up in the lungs, which makes it more difficult for the lungs to collect oxygen. Pulmonary fibrosis is less common than asthma, bronchitis or emphysema.

WHAT IS A PULMONARY PROGRAM?

"In this country we tend to treat lung disease, a chronic condition, as an acute illness," Tiep says. "We're real good at taking care of problems once they become apparent to us, but we haven't been very good at working to prevent those problems."

The focus in the past has been to put a person suffering from lung disease on medication (such as inhaled bronchodilators) and send them home. As the disease progresses, the dosage or the type of medication may change for the patient, but little else does. A person suffering from advanced lung disease—someone who is most at risk for multiple hospitalizations—is the patient most likely to be referred to a pulmonary program.

Pulmonary programs were developed to mount a comprehensive approach to caring for a patient suffering from lung disease, an attack plan that mixes medicine with management. These programs bring together such elements as patient education, prevention methods (such as smoking cessation), exercise and diet. Ideally, pulmonary programs deal with the whole picture and not just specific symptoms.

Goals

It is important for patients and their family members to remember that a chronic condition like lung disease means just that—*chronic*. There is no cure! It's not going away. Acceptance of that fact is indeed the first step for a person (and their loved ones) entering a pulmonary program. The primary goals of a pulmonary program are to help a person breathe better, breathe easier and to reduce the impact of the disease on the life of the patient and his family. Through education and training, a person with lung disease can eliminate a lot of the fear, uncertainty and depression that is often associated with the disease.

THE PULMONARY TEAM

A comprehensive pulmonary program usually utilizes various members of a hospital's medical staff for its team. While a doctor coordinates the program, an array of therapists, nurses and other support staff work directly with the patients on a day-to-day basis. Some hospitals may offer a pulmonary program that uses only a variation of these teams, while others may add different components.

Respiratory Therapist

A respiratory therapist is the key player on a pulmonary team. This person teaches you how and when to take your medications and your oxygen (if you are on oxygen). They also administer chest physical therapy (which can include massaging and beating on the chest to help knock excess phlegm loose so it can be coughed up). They also help you develop the appropriate posture to ensure better breathing.

Physician

A doctor serves as medical director of a pulmonary program, coordinating treatment plans for patients and overseeing the operation of the team. Tiep notes, however, that a doctor's actual daily involvement in the program will vary from program to program. Some doctors make daily rounds among the patients (including those seen on an outpatient basis), while others may only hold weekly briefings to go over charts and confer with staff. Ultimately, the doctor is the one who will make the determination if a program is working for a patient.

Physical Therapist

This team member works with you on exercises that will build your strength, endurance and stamina—all key elements in fighting lung disease.

Occupational Therapist

This team member helps you with functional training, including leisure activities, personal activities (bathing, etc.) and work activities.

Dietitian

The joke is that this team member is going to teach you how to eat food that doesn't taste good. The reality is that people suffering from lung disease often shy away from food, because the process of eating can make them short of breath. Subsequently, they become undernourished, which can eventually lead to other complications. A dietitian educates you about how and what to eat, as well as what not to eat if you are suffering from lung disease. Most people with COPD are told to stick with a low sodium diet.

Social Worker

This team player helps you and your family cope with the serious and widespread impact that lung disease can have on a family. Depression and anxiety attacks often plague people with lung disease. A social worker can refer you and your family to support groups and identify other means of assistance that are available. They are also there to listen when you simply need someone to talk to.

HOW A PULMONARY PROGRAM WORKS

Pulmonary programs are a lot like the high school classes that teach teens how to drive: Education is the first step. Training comes second. "A good pulmonary program will teach you how to operate your body," Tiep says. "Better maintenance means better performance."

If you are admitted to a pulmonary program on an inpatient basis, you might receive up to eight hours of therapy and training each day. Through an outpatient program, you are likely to be attending program classes for two to three hours-a-day, two to three days-a-week. Tiep estimates an average pulmonary program will last four to eight weeks. Some programs can last as long as 12 weeks, though that is more rare.

During the first stages of the education process, patients learn more about their disease and how accepting the diagnosis is key to being able to manage the symptoms and reclaim an active life. This is an extremely important part of the process, Tiep notes, because without such intervention many people with lung disease simply withdraw further into an inactive and reclusive lifestyle. "These are people who get short of breath doing anything, therefore they don't do anything. By not doing anything, they grow weaker and are eventually unable to do anything or go anywhere," he says. "It's a vicious spiral."

A pulmonary program will work to instill (or strengthen) a sense of independence in patients, helping temper the idea that when a person is sick they must rely on others to take care of them. Patient empowerment and responsibility are a big part of the program.

Self-Assessment and Monitoring

Since much of a pulmonary patient's regimen will be carried out on their own at home, they are trained to be studious record-keepers of their progress. This is very important, as changes in shortness of breath, discharge of phlegm and the nature of a cough all need to be monitored on a daily basis. A person will generally chart themselves in a simple manner, such as "Breathing: Better, Same or Worse than the day before?" A person can measure their shortness of breath at home by counting out loud to 20 immediately after they finish exercising. How many breaths they have to take during that count will determine where they're at on the scale (i.e., counting to 20 on one breath is Level 1, taking two breaths is Level 2, etc.).

Monitoring your mucous discharge (also called "clearing your secretions") is also very important. The body produces mucous to coat its airways and to help prevent infections from bacteria. A person with lung disease produces excessive amounts of mucous and has a more difficult time clearing it. During the monitoring process at home, a patient will note whether the mucous they are clearing is thin and light or thick and dark or the same as the day before.

Evaluations should occur at the same time each day, to help ensure consistency. Many people with lung disease discover that one particular time of the day can be more difficult for them (typically in the morning) while another time can be much better for them (often in the evening). A person's record of their own progress is then available to their doctor and their respiratory therapist, who will get a much more detailed picture of day-to-day progress.

Exercise

Exercising plays a central role for the pulmonary patient. It builds strength, endurance and confidence while reducing stress and anxiety. "If a pulmonary program is the vehicle to a better life for a person with lung disease, then exercise is the engine that powers the vehicle," Tiep says, noting that exercise remains the most effective way to reduce shortness of breath in the long run.

Continuous walking—usually not on a treadmill—is a hallmark pulmonary exercise. Arm exercises are also important. People with lung disease often have difficulty in raising their arms higher than shoulder level. As this trouble increases, it inhibits daily activities that require one to reach above their shoulders (think about that: everything from combing your hair to grabbing a glass out of the cabinet is a strain!). A pulmonary program will give patients exercises called "gravity resistive exercises" to help build their arm strength and endurance. These detailed exercises are closely paced with a person's individual breathing rate.

Clearing Phlegm

Getting rid of the excess mucous that builds up in a patient's airways is important. A pulmonary program will teach a person different methods to clear their airways. As you might imagine, coughing is the most effective method, but in a pulmonary program a person will learn the best way to cough it out. A program will also introduce the patient to things that help loosen the phlegm, such as warm liquids, chest vibrators, and inhalers that contain medication which open the airways (called bronchodilators).

Oxygen

Many people with lung disease rely upon oxygen from a tank, as their lungs are not collecting enough to meet their body's needs. Whether or not a person is getting enough oxygen cannot always be determined by the mere fact that they are out of breath. A person with lung disease will be tested to find out if they need additional oxygen and, if so, what delivery method will work best for them.

Nutrition

A pulmonary program will stress a low sodium diet, as salt can lead to higher blood pressure, swelling, and additional stress on the heart and lungs. As noted above, lung disease patients (especially those not in a pulmonary program) are at risk of being undernourished because eating can often cause shortness of breath; therefore, the patients are often reluctant to eat. On the other end of the spectrum are overweight people who have lung disease. This presents another potentially dangerous situation, since obesity places a greater strain on the heart and lungs. Customized diets, created with the help of a dietitian, are an integral part of a pulmonary program.

Lifestyle Changes

As smoking (both primary and second-hand) is the number one cause of chronic lung disease in America, a successful pulmonary program will help its patients who still smoke with smoking cessation programs. Such programs are fairly widespread today and are open to people who don't have lung disease (yet) and wish to quit smoking.

People with lung disease also often suffer from bouts of insomnia. A pulmonary program will offer alternatives to sleeping pills, which can be dangerous and addictive.

QUESTIONS TO ASK AND THINGS TO CONSIDER

According to Tiep, most primary care physicians are not completely familiar with a comprehensive pulmonary program, so the likelihood that your doctor will direct you to one is slim. It's up to you to ask your doctor what he knows about pulmonary programs and whether or not he can refer you to one in your area. If he can't, you may ask him to refer you to a pulmonary specialist who can.

Tiep says people looking for a pulmonary program should consider the following questions during their search:

▶ Does the program offer a support group? It should, as this is a very important part of the pulmonary rehabilitation process. A support group plugs you into a host of other valuable resources. Attend a meeting of the program's support group to see how it operates. Ask members of the support group how the program has worked for them, what sort of problems they've had in the program, how it has changed their life and whether or not they would recommend it.

▶ Is the program operated out of a hospital? It should be, as a hospital is more likely to offer a greater degree of comprehensive care and a team approach.

▶ How big is the program? Most programs average between 6 to 10 patients, which (depending on the staff size) allows for a greater degree of interaction between staff and patients.

▶ Who runs the program? Is the medical director a pulmonary specialist? How much experience has the respiratory therapist had and where has he worked?

▶ Is there is patient guidebook? A program that uses a patient guidebook is a plus. Guidebooks help patients focus on narrow, important pieces of information and, as a practical matter, are a useful resource when working on the program at home. It gives you something to work with.

Tiep sums up a good pulmonary program as one which not only helps its patients gain as much control over their disease as possible, but one that also helps turn them into providers of their own health care—men and women who see their doctors more as a good advisor and less as a savior.

CHAPTER 12

The Neurology Unit: Brain Central

> **Patient:** "I know there is a move
> to outpatient treatment, but are you sure
> my primary care doctor is authorized
> to do brain surgery in his office?"
> **Receptionist:** "I'm not sure, but with only a
> $5 co-payment, why not give it a shot?"
>
> **JOKE FOUND ON THE INTERNET**

There are few if any types of medicine more complex than neurology. While other systems in the body involve essentially basic mechanical functions (i.e., pumps and valves, etc.), the brain is a massive and complex information processor, much of which is still a mystery.

To highlight how complex the field is—and how rapidly

doctors are learning more about the human brain—consider that it has been said that the sum knowledge of neurosciences is doubling every six years, meaning that textbooks written just a few years ago are now out of date.

BIGGER CAN MEAN BETTER

Neurologists and neurosurgeons are highly skilled specialists who usually operate out of larger medical centers or teaching hospitals which have greater access to state-of-the-art equipment. Mid-size to smaller hospitals are less likely to have separate units and will probably integrate neurology patients into a standard wing or transfer them out to a larger facility.

As a consumer, there are a few basic things you should know about a neurology unit.

"Those two are lawsuits just waiting to happen!"

There are a variety of conditions that are going to land you in a neurology unit, including neurological infections (such as encephalitis and meningitis), brain or spinal cord tumors, diseases such as Multiple Sclerosis (MS) and Lou Gehrig's disease, vascular disease (strokes), brain trauma (from accidents, etc.), epilepsy, and various developmental disorders and viruses.

John Freeland, a psychologist with specialty training in neuropsychology (study of the psychological and cognitive effects of neurological injury), says patients and their families should consider a variety of issues when looking for the appropriate neurological care.

A primary concern will be how urgent the situation is, which will determine how much time you have to select a neurologist. Some conditions are going to get you into a neurology unit immediately, like brain trauma or if you suffer an acute onset of diplopia (the condition where one eye starts looking another direction, sort of a rapid and extreme version of "lazy eye"). In these instances, your primary care doctor is more than likely going to refer you immediately to a neurologist.

EARLY DIAGNOSIS

Freeland notes that one of the biggest risks today are people with neurological disorders who are not diagnosed soon enough. Primary care doctors are often pressed to treat patients without referring them to specialists. Thus, the early warning signs—headaches, memory loss, concentration problems, fatigue and other non-specific complaints—may not be properly interpreted.

As doctors face increased pressure to defer referrals to specialists until absolutely necessary, it is vital that you remain vigilant and request a specialist if you feel you are not getting the answers or the treatment you need.

Freeland says patients should tap into as many resources as possible when diagnosed with a neurological disorder, including patient advocacy groups, referral lines and the internet, which has become a great medical resource.

QUESTIONS TO ASK AND THINGS TO CONSIDER

If you have time, however—for instance if you are dealing with a slow-growing brain tumor—then Freeland suggests you ask your doctor or the neurologist the following questions:

▸ If I have time to "shop around," how much time do I have? How soon does this have to be treated?

▸ Is there a subspecialty for the disorder I have? If your child has a brain tumor, for example, are you getting referred to a pediatric neuro-oncologist? If not, where is the nearest hospital with a pediatric neuro-oncology unit and what is the practicality of using them? You should also consult with your health insurance company.

▶ If there is not a subspecialty for the disorder you or a loved one is suffering from, there are usually neurologists who have greater levels of experience in dealing with that particular disorder. Ask your neurologist or your primary care doctor (before he makes the referral) how much experience the neurologist has with this disorder. For example, some neurologists are very experienced in interpreting EEGs, a test that determines the presence of epilepsy.

▶ Ask your neurologist what the alternatives are to the course of treatment he has recommended and what the risks are by not pursuing the course of treatment immediately or at all. Determine the pros and cons of each treatment option.

▶ Ask your neurologist if there could be other explanations for the symptoms from which you are suffering. How strong are the indicators for your diagnosis and how did he reach it?

▶ Can the neurologist or the hospital he is working out of recommend consumer organizations that deal with your specific condition? Today, there are consumer information organizations that can provide you with very valuable information about your condition and plug you into networks of people who also have the same diagnosis. These clearinghouses of information will provide you with additional details of the pros and cons of treatments as well as background information on various medical centers that treat your condition.

▸ If you are facing neurosurgery, make sure that you have access to a nurse practitioner or a physician's assistant who can explain the surgery and its risks and benefits, as neurosurgeons are notoriously busy with exceedingly tight schedules. You have a right to this information and the neurosurgeon may in fact meet with you to debrief you on the operation. However, getting even 20 minutes with these surgeons can be difficult, therefore a qualified surrogate becomes very important.

The Intensive Care Unit: A Hospital's SWAT Team

"The optimist has a better chance for
health than the pessimist."

FLOYD W. PARSONS

An intensive care unit (ICU) is probably one of the most technically advanced and well-staffed sections of any hospital. It's also one of the last places you or your loved ones want to be.

Medically, the bottom line is this: If you are admitted to an ICU, it essentially means your illness or injury is so serious that normal hospital staffing levels, monitoring and treatments are not enough to ensure your survival.

You might consider an ICU to be the hospital's version of a police department's SWAT unit—in that they both deploy specially-trained teams in concentrated numbers to attack potentially deadly problems. You or a loved one may end up in an ICU following a car crash (once the emergency room has stabilized your condition) or you may be cycled through an ICU following surgery. No matter how you arrive at an ICU, once you are there it is important that your family members and loved ones understand what the unit does, how it functions, who staffs an ICU and what a family and patient can expect while they are there.

THE INTENSIVE CARE UNIT: WHAT IS IT?

An ICU is designed to accommodate the very seriously ill and injured. These patients need a much more intense level of treatment intervention—such as life-support systems—as well as nursing care that's overseen by a critical care physician.

The rooms in an ICU are usually packed with hi-tech equipment, such as ventilators (which essentially breathe for you), machines that monitor heart and blood pressure, feeding equipment and more.

Patients who are admitted to an ICU are likely to be hooked up to a variety of these machines, which are equipped with a system of alarms and buzzers that signal nursing staff whenever there is a critical change in the patient.

The hospital's SWAT team:
"No need to worry ma'am, we're specialists!"

If your blood pressure drops, an IV line clogs or your heart rate becomes erratic, alarms will sound.

As an example of the intense level of nursing and monitoring that goes on in an ICU, consider that life-support machines will sound different types of alarms for various levels of the same medical occurrence: a machine that monitors a patient's blood pressure will emit a buzzing noise if there is a mild or slight change in the patient's blood pressure, while a more dramatic shift in blood pressure will trigger a louder alarm. In this way, ICU nurses remain constantly apprised of even the slightest changes in a patient's condition.

ICUS: MANY SHAPES AND SIZES

Intensive care units vary in size and focus. Some hospitals have ICUs that will treat all patients with life-threatening conditions. Other hospitals, especially larger medical centers, categorize their ICUs. These hospitals may have a traditional ICU, as well as a pediatric ICU, a neonatal ICU, a cardiac ICU (or a coronary care unit—CCU) and a surgical ICU.

A neonatal ICU specializes in treating newborn babies who are suffering from all sorts of life-threatening conditions. An infant's needs (from fluids, temperature, oxygen and more) are far different than an adult's. A pediatric ICU focuses on children and teens. A cardiac ICU or a CCU is geared toward patients who have either just suffered a heart attack or have come out of open heart surgery. Surgical ICU handles patients who have had complications in surgery. The common thread through each of these different categories is the level of treatment and the emphasis on critical care by staff.

There is no such thing as privacy in an ICU unit. Unlike other hospital rooms, there are no toilets, sinks or showers. The bathroom is a bedpan and the bath is a bucket and sponge. Don't count on sending a lot of flowers to a person in an ICU or bringing them the sort of personal effects you would normally find in other hospital rooms, as most hospitals severely restrict such items in an ICU.

WHO WORKS IN AN ICU?

Doctors

An Intensive Care Unit is usually staffed by doctors who specialize in critical care, an area of medicine which requires board certification. According to Dr. John B. Sampson, who operates a web site that details the workings of an ICU, a physician who is certified in critical care medicine has completed fellowship-level training in the field and has passed a national examination. Fellowship training in critical care provides the doctor with experience in life support, treatment of infectious diseases, heart failure, respiratory failure and shock. Sampson explains that critical care is considered a subspecialty field in medicine, so doctors must first be board certified in anesthesiology, internal medicine, pediatrics or surgery before they can become certified in critical care. The majority of critical care doctors today have backgrounds in internal medicine. Critical care doctors should have no outpatient commitments that might conflict with their duties in an ICU, and Sampson notes that hospitals should staff ICUs in such a manner that critical care doctors are available around-the-clock, seven days-a-week. Surprisingly, Sampson says that most hospitals that have ICUs don't provide that kind of coverage by critical care doctors and that many hospitals have doctors working in their ICUs who are not board certified in the critical care field.

Nurses

As with most other units of a hospital, nurses make up the backbone of the staff in an ICU. Like doctors staffing an ICU, these nurses are often trained in critical care, which means they've passed a national ICU exam and have ICU experience. While their peers in other sections of the hospital are usually working with much higher patient-to-nurse ratios, the ICU nurse deals with ratios that can be as low as one-on-one or even two nurses to one patient. This is due to the fact that ICU patients are often extremely unstable and require constant and focused nursing.

ICUs are also supported by the staff that operates the hospital as a whole, such as administrators, social workers, chaplains and others.

WHAT SORT OF PATIENTS ARE TREATED IN AN ICU?

As stated at the beginning of this chapter, ICUs treat people who are in a very serious medical situation, either as a result of injury or illness, and whose survival depends on constant monitoring and intense treatment interventions—such as life-support. Constant visual contact between the nurse and the patient is critical.

Accordingly, ICUs see just about every sort of patient you can imagine, from burn victims and people who have been injured in car or motorcycle accidents to those patients who have battled long illnesses such as cancer, heart or lung disease.

Dr. Ron Perkin, Director of the Pediatric Intensive Care Unit at Loma Linda University Children's Hospital, says the hospital's PICU has 25 beds and treats about 150 patients each month. Of those patients, who range in age from one month to 18-years-old, nearly two-thirds have suffered some sort of trauma or accident, Perkin says. The remaining third are struggling with chronic illnesses.

HOW AN ICU FUNCTIONS
AND WHAT TO EXPECT

Walking into an ICU to visit a loved one can be quite a shock to many families who are unprepared. Katy Dalke, the Nurse Manager for PICU at Loma Linda University's Children's Hospital, says parents are often stunned when they arrive to find their child "hooked up" to an array of machines that are humming and buzzing with flashing lights. The shock can deepen when parents see their child not responding to their touch or the sound of their voice.

Accordingly, ICU staff members will usually try to intercept parents or family members before they see their loved one, Dalke says. This allows staff members the opportunity to explain the patient's condition and prepare family members for what they can expect to see.

The layout, staffing and visitation policies for ICUs will obviously vary from hospital to hospital. Dalke notes that at Loma Linda the PICU is laid out in single-bed rooms, which allows for a greater degree of privacy for the patient and family. Perkin notes that most of the nation's 200-plus PICUs are laid out with two-bed rooms and some will feature a single, large ward with a dozen or more beds. Most PICUs (and ICUs) will also have an "Infection Room"—a single-bed room where a patient fighting an infectious disease is isolated to protect other patients in the unit.

Visitation policy at Loma Linda's PICU allows for no more than two family members at a time in the room, as a patient and even staff might be overwhelmed with a large group of family members surrounding the bed. Family members must check in at the nurse's station when coming to see a patient; they cannot just walk into the room. Family members are generally not allowed to sleep in the ICU rooms. While parents and grandparents are allowed freely into a PICU room, Dalke says Loma Linda requires child siblings to be accompanied by a Child Life Specialist. This staff member helps explain to the sibling what is happening with their brother or sister.

In the event of an emergency, family members are not allowed in the room and if they are in the room when it occurs, they are expected to leave. Medical staff have to be free to focus on what's happening with the patient, not with the emotional reactions of family members.

Families are likely to notice the high level of nursing that takes place in an ICU, where nurse to patient ratios can be as low as one-to-one. The nursing assignments for each patient are determined by how many procedures the person needs during treatment, the degree of supervision and any complications the patient may have, Dalke says. At Loma Linda, PICU nurses pull a standard 12-hour shift, three days-a-week.

The average length of stay for patients in Loma Linda's PICU is about four days, which Perkin says is close to the national average.

A family can often become accustomed to this intense level of nursing and Dalke says staff will prepare a family when their loved one is getting transferred to what's known as a "step-down" unit—a ward which provides a level of care between an ICU and the standard acute care units. In a step-down unit, patients are no longer on life-support systems. Nurses are trained in ICU observational skills but they handle a slightly higher ratio of patients, probably two or three per nurse. A step-down unit will have far less equipment in the room and in most cases there will be two beds or more in a room.

Dalke says family members are often ruffled when they see less and less of a nurse, but she notes that actually it should be considered good news, as the patient is requiring a less intense level of care—also known as "getting better." The average length of stay for patients in Loma Linda's step-down unit is about five days.

How to Stay Informed While in an ICU

When a person is being treated in an ICU, numerous doctors may take part in a coordinated effort to save their lives. Watching a parade of specialists hover over the bed of a loved one, examining charts and murmuring to each other in low tones, can be rather confusing and even alarming to family members.

In an emergency situation, medical staff members obviously don't have time to explain everything that is happening. Other than emergencies, however, you have a right to know *who* is seeing your loved one, *what* role they are playing in their treatment, and *why* they are involved.

The primary care doctor, who is coordinating the treatment, will often fill you in on what's happening. The ICU shift nurse will also be a good source of information. If you feel you are in the dark about the care your family member is receiving, don't hesitate to ask the primary care doctor or one of the nurses. You may also have the opportunity to speak with the specialists who, in fact, will often seek you out to give you an update on your loved one's condition.

Second Opinions

If you wish to seek an outside opinion or bring in another specialist while you or a family member is being treated in an ICU, you should talk with the physician who is coordinating ICU care. Express your wishes to him and, if such treatment is approved, he will make arrangements for the outside physician to see the patient.

Dalke says that patients can also be transferred to another hospital's ICU for treatment, but that arrangements will have to be made with the respective medical staffs at each hospital. If you have questions about this, talk with the charge nurse or the director of the ICU.

Often times when a person is in serious or critical condition, their family can become desperate to do something more to help them, particularly if they are not responding well to traditional medical treatments. Under such circumstances, some families understandably ask to use an alternative or complimentary medical therapy on their loved one while he or she is still in the hospital.

In general, hospitals tend to be hesitant to allow alternative therapies to be used on a patient under their care. For the most part, this is a legal concern. If the patient were to die while receiving treatment from a doctor not licensed by the state, the hospital could be considered liable for that death.

Dalke points out that families should consult with their primary care doctor and the ICU director if they desire an alternative therapy. One patient of hers, Dalke recalls, sought treatment with herbal medicine. The request was reviewed and approved by the hospital's chief of medical staff. However, when the patient responded negatively to the alternative treatment, the therapy was immediately stopped.

Dalke notes that requests for alternative treatments will probably be reviewed at the highest levels of a hospital's medical staff before approval is granted.

Other Special Care Units

While nearly every hospital has at least a standard ICU, other larger hospitals have developed a range of special care units that are designed to treat various types of trauma. These units include burn centers and neurological injury units, which are staffed by physicians who specialize in the needs of people who have been badly burned or have suffered a traumatic brain or spinal cord injury.

LIVING WILLS

Simply put, a living will is the best, most legally sound way of letting hospital medical staff know what your wishes are regarding efforts to save your life (i.e., should you be placed on life support) and whether or not to "pull the plug." A standard version of a living will is a simple document that requests no "heroic measures" be used to save your life and that if there are no *reasonable* expectations of recovery from illness or injury that the person be allowed to die with dignity. If you or a loved one are going into the hospital for serious treatment (i.e., major surgery), you should make sure the hospital is aware of your living will prior to treatment—ideally at the time of admission. If you or a loved one are there as a result of an unexpected emergency, the person responsible (your "proxy") for your health care decisions should have a copy available to them to present to medical staff as evidence of your wishes.

INFORMED CONSENT

When in the hospital or undergoing medical treatment, patients have the right to what's known as "informed consent" (with the notable exception of an emergency). In essence, this is exactly what it sounds like: in order to willfully agree to undergo a medical treatment or procedure, you must understand what is going to happen during the procedure and treatment, what the risks are and what the potential outcomes are. Informed consent is sought prior to treatment (and sedation) and you must sign a document noting that consent was sought and given.

QUESTIONS TO ASK AND THINGS TO CONSIDER

As Sampson notes, "By the time you need to go to an ICU, it is probably too late to be choosy." That's why it is important to be aware of your options before you get sick or injured, particularly if you or your family are in an HMO that dictates from which hospital you will be receiving critical care.

It's also important to remember that patients can indeed be transferred from one ICU to another, so if you feel that another ICU offers more appropriate care it is possible to move a patient.

As noted before, Sampson points out that many ICUs are staffed by medical doctors who are not board certified critical care physicians. Sampson encourages you to ask if the hospital has critical care doctors and nurses who are board certified. If the hospital does not have any critical care certified doctors, ask who manages the ICU. Will your own primary care physician be expected to manage you in the ICU via telephone if he is at home or at the clinic?

Some of the other questions that Sampson says people should consider when evaluating a hospital's ICU are:

▶ If the hospital has certified critical care doctors, do they see every patient who goes into the ICU?

▶ Are critical care doctors available 24 hours-a-day, seven days-a-week?

▶ Are nurses in the ICU certified in Advanced Cardiac Life Support?

▶ What percentage of the nurses in the hospital's ICU are certified in critical care?

▶ Does the hospital's ICU have a social worker who specializes in critical care cases?

▸ Does the hospital have a pediatric ICU or do they have a standard ICU that treats children as well as adults?

▸ If they have a pediatric ICU, are the doctors board certified in pediatric critical care?

▸ What are the ICU visitation policies and hours? Is around-the-clock visitation permitted? What is the hospital's policy on ICU sleepovers? What housing arrangements can be made through the hospital if the family needs to stay at or near the facility?

These questions and others about an ICU can be asked of the charge nurse in the unit or you can simply call the hospital's community relations officer. You may even consider getting the fax number for the hospital's community relations department (this would be available by calling the front desk) and faxing over a list of specific questions. You may also ask for any patient handbooks the hospital publishes. These publications usually have sections on ICUs and are good sources for the hospital's standard procedures.

Rehabilitation: On the Road Again...

"Sickness comes on horseback,
but goes away on foot."

W.C. HAZLITT

One of the most critical things a person should know about the health care system today is the availability and importance of medical rehabilitation. When most people hear the word "rehabilitation" they immediately associate it with either a drug detoxification program or something that's supposed to happen to criminals while they are behind bars.

But medical rehabilitation is actually a host of specialized treatment disciplines that help people recover from a traumatic injury or illness. Medical rehabilitation includes physical therapy, occupational therapy, recreational therapy, speech therapy, pain management and more. It's important that you know a little about rehabilitation because most Americans, at some point in their lives, will suffer some sort of disabling injury or illness that will require some form of rehabilitation therapy.

Yet unless a person has suffered such an injury or illness, or knows someone who has, chances are they know very little about rehabilitation, where it's offered, how to get it, what it entails, who is entitled to it and how it is paid for.

Indeed, since many Americans are unfamiliar with rehabilitation, most of us have a peculiar notion about what it takes to recover from a serious injury or illness.

GETTING BETTER IS HARD WORK

This lack of understanding is repeatedly reinforced by Hollywood's depictions of shooting victims, car accident victims, and people who suffer strokes, heart attacks and lung disease. Movies and television usually portray people recovering from a traumatic injury as undergoing what in reality would be considered a miracle: a shooting victim is rushed to the hospital, where ER docs save his life and stabilize his condition, though it's determined his spinal cord has been badly damaged. Then, by the magic of Hollywood—and the necessity of steering clear of tedious plot developments—the person either mounts a full recovery in the general hospital (seemingly in a matter of days), or is sent home to recuperate in bed (where we are led to believe everything from a broken leg to brain damage can be healed with a good night's sleep and lots of juice).

While some cinematic depictions are becoming more medically accurate, Hollywood's impact on the perception of how people get better can't be overstated. Literally millions of Americans discover the hard way every year that recovering from a life-altering injury or illness requires relentless work, dedication and perseverance from the patient and an array of therapists. People who face extensive rehabilitation following an injury or illness are often stunned to learn what it takes to "get better." Some people are so overwhelmed by the prospect that they go into denial, which only worsens their situation.

A FULL CONTINUUM OF CARE

The good news is that America today has one of the most advanced medical rehabilitation systems in the world. A full continuum of care, from inpatient therapy to transitional care is available to help ease a patient back into everyday life. Even better news is that more people are learning about rehabilitation and the more educated people are about rehabilitation, the better they will be able to use the health care system to their advantage.

Yet the tough reality remains that getting better can take weeks, months and sometimes years. And sometimes a person never fully recovers. In such cases, rehabilitation becomes even more critical, as it helps patients achieve their functional potential and recapture as much of their life as possible.

REHABILITATION: THE FIRST STEP

Many people first learn about medical rehabilitation from their doctor while they are still in an acute care hospital. While it is often a serious injury or illness that landed them there, doctors will often recommend rehabilitation for much less serious injuries, such as a broken arm or leg or arthritis, usually on an outpatient basis.

When a person suffers a serious injury or illness, it is likely they will be transferred to a rehabilitation facility as soon as they're medically stable. As more hospitals either already have or are developing their own rehabilitation units, being transferred may just mean moving down the hall or to a different floor in the same building. Other hospitals work with centers that specialize exclusively in providing rehabilitation, in which case a person may be transferred to a different facility altogether.

Casa Colina Centers for Rehabilitation in Pomona, California, is a good example of a "stand alone" facility that specializes exclusively in providing a wide array of rehabilitation services. Established in 1936 to help children who were recovering from polio, Casa Colina has grown to meet people's changing rehabilitation needs. As polio disappeared with the advent of vaccines, Casa Colina turned its focus to helping people recover from other debilitating injuries and illnesses. Today the facility offers a full continuum of rehabilitation services, from a 66-bed hospital that specializes in rehabilitation medicine to myriad programs that ease a person's transition back into life at home and work.

INPATIENT REHABILITATION

Depending on the severity of a patient's medical condition and what level of care they require, a person recovering from a traumatic injury or illness is likely to be transferred into a facility that provides either acute or subacute care (skilled nursing) or both. In the inpatient treatment setting, a person will have a hospital room much like the room he had at the general hospital. The difference is the patient will leave the room several times a day to undergo a regimen of therapy. The setting for the therapy may be a gym decked out with specialized equipment, a treatment pool, or just a plain room that looks more like an office. It all depends on what kind of therapy the person needs. Following the day's therapy, the patient will return to his room, where he can be monitored and cared for by the medical staff. As his condition improves, he will be evaluated and eventually discharged to continue with outpatient therapy. As with general hospitals, the length of stays in rehabilitation hospitals or centers has been dramatically reduced as a result of efforts to contain costs.

OUTPATIENT REHABILITATION

Once a person has recovered some of their strength, coordination, balance, mobility and other abilities that may have been limited by their injury or illness, they will be discharged. However, they are likely to continue their rehabilitation therapy on an outpatient basis.

This simply means they will be living at home again, but will return to the rehabilitation facility on a regular schedule, such as three or five days-a-week. Sessions can last from two hours to an entire day. The goal is to advance the gains a person made during their inpatient therapy.

A greater emphasis is now placed on outpatient rehabilitation. One obvious reason for this is that it is less expensive to deliver. However, it is also in most people's best interest to get back into their home and community environment as soon as possible, which outpatient therapy allows. Just how much outpatient therapy a person receives will depend upon their need and what their insurance will cover.

BASIC REHABILITATION PROGRAMS

A rehabilitation provider is likely to offer a variety of general programs for people recovering from specific injuries or illnesses. Once admitted into a general program, a person will undergo treatment that is crafted to their specific needs.

Some of the more common rehabilitation programs include: spinal cord injury, brain injury, pulmonary rehabilitation, and stroke and pain management. Other rehabilitation programs assist people recovering from orthopedic conditions, amputations and burns. Many rehabilitation providers offer programs that are tailored for children. These providers integrate children's special needs with the therapy process and work closely with their parents.

TREATMENT TEAM MEMBERS

Rehabilitation facilities that offer comprehensive services are generally staffed with an array of skilled therapists who work together as a team to meet a patient's wide-ranging needs. A patient who has suffered a spinal cord injury, for example, may be treated by a physical therapist in the morning, undergo occupational therapy in the early afternoon,

"My rehab is going pretty well…
I think I've got my frog's legs back!"

meet with a psychologist in the late afternoon and talk with a social worker that evening. Once or twice a week the same patient may work with a recreation therapist. The following is a brief introduction to some of the team members a person going through rehabilitation may encounter:

Physical Therapist (PT)

The physical therapist can be seen as a coach or a personal trainer. Their goal is to help a patient recover the strength, balance, flexibility, coordination, mobility and endurance that was lost as a result of the injury or illness. Like a good coach, the PT will also teach exercises that the patient will be able to use at home or even work, so that the therapeutic work will continue even after the program has officially ended.

Occupational Therapist (OT)

The occupational therapist should not be confused with a job coach, as they are more like a *life* coach. The OT's main responsibilities are helping a patient relearn and recover the skills required in day-to-day life that may have been taken away as a result of the injury or illness. The OT will focus on a patient's coordination, balance, body control, self-care needs and visual perception. Like the PT, the OT will help a person learn strategies they will be able to apply outside of the formal therapy setting, when they are essentially on their own.

Recreation Therapist (RT)

The "rec therapist," as they are often called, is not a travel agent-turned-vacation guru, but rather a highly trained professional who helps a patient reenter the community and reestablish or even improve their previous quality of life. As people with disabilities and functional limitations are demanding and receiving more access to every aspect of our society today, the RT's job has taken on an even greater importance. The RT helps a person adapt or modify the leisure activities they enjoyed prior to the injury or illness. The RT can also help with critical social readjustments.

Speech Therapist

Communicating skills can be dramatically affected by certain injuries or illnesses, such as a stroke. During the recovery process, a speech therapist helps a patient improve their communication skills by overcoming whatever memory, language, speech and hearing problems are hindering effective communication.

Psychologist

The emotional wounds that are caused by a major illness or injury can be as devastating to the person as the physical damage. Unlike the physical injury, emotional duress can and usually does spread to families and loved ones. A psychologist can help the patient and his or her family make the major adjustments in their lives that are often necessary.

The psychologist helps a patient recover their sexuality, self-esteem and self-image.

Social Worker

The social worker fills in the critical gaps, helping patients regain control over their personal and financial lives. Social workers generally work to make the transition from hospital to rehab center to home go smoothly. Social workers can refer patients to a wide variety of useful services and programs. (See chapter seven for a better idea of the services a social worker can provide.)

BEYOND THE HOSPITAL'S DOORS

A popular saying among rehabilitation providers is "Rehabilitation doesn't stop at the hospital's doors." Fortunately for Americans, this phrase is becoming more and more true, as people with disabilities are establishing themselves in every aspect of society. They are doing so with the help of rehabilitation programs that are no longer designed to simply get a person well enough to move them out of the hospital doors and back home to their bed or sofa.

Rehabilitation is—and should be—about getting back to work, back to school, back into sports, back into life. It's about being a whole person again.

To that end, a patient facing rehabilitation therapy should be aware of services and programs that many facilities offer which will help them recover as much of their life as possible. The wide range of community reentry programs available include the following:

Wheelchair Sports

A person who becomes a wheelchair-user following an injury or illness no longer has to be content to sit in front of a television or on the sidelines, soaking up sports vicariously. Wheelchair sports are booming around the nation, with literally thousands of teams competing in basketball, hockey, rugby (also known as "murder ball" because it's as rough as the able-bodied version), tennis and power soccer. Many rehabilitation facilities offer a full wheelchair sports program that feature workshops, training and regular practices in a variety of sports. Chances are they also sponsor teams that play in local, regional and national leagues. Most of these programs are free.

Outdoor Programs

The great outdoors is simply that: great. A person who has a functional limitation no longer has to watch the Discovery Channel in order to check out exotic locales. More rehabilitation centers today are offering programs that facilitate trips for people of all abilities into the wild. Such programs can include white-water rafting, dog-sledding, camping, rock climbing, horseback riding and sailing. There are even programs which offer adapted scuba diving (a six week course taught by experts which fully credentials people with disabilities as certified divers) and assisted kayaking.

Like wheelchair sports, these programs work with an individual's specific needs to find out what activities are right for them. The programs are generally free, though sometimes involve a nominal fee to cover the cost of the trip. Scholarships are also often available.

Career Development Programs

Getting back to work is vital to a person's self-esteem and self-image following a debilitating injury or illness. Sometimes a person recovers enough to assume their old job again. Other times they may need to find a new job that is better suited to their abilities following rehabilitation. There are many programs available which help people return to their old jobs or train for, find and keep new ones. It's important to find out what sort of return-to-work services a rehabilitation facility offers.

Disabled Driver Programs

Once a person is prepared to move back into social and career activities, being able to drive is critical. There are clear economic, emotional and psychological benefits to driving. Thanks to technology, people who could not drive because of functional limitations just a decade ago can now, with proper training and licensing, get behind the wheel.

Many rehabilitation facilities offer disabled driver programs, which provide functional assessment, behind-the-wheel evaluations and equipment training. Such programs work closely with the Department of Motor Vehicles. Many facilities charge for these programs, but some insurance companies will pay for them.

QUESTIONS TO ASK AND THINGS TO CONSIDER

As with most serious medical situations, it is critical that a patient or their family members question their doctor thoroughly before being transferred for rehabilitation. A doctor should discuss a variety of issues with them regarding the rehabilitation he is recommending and the facility where the patient will be receiving the treatment.

Some questions you should ask your doctor:

▶ Why did you choose that facility for the rehabilitation you are prescribing?

▶ Have you referred many patients there?

▶ Do you specialize in the kind of rehabilitation therapy I need?

▶ How long will I receive inpatient therapy?

▶ What sort of outpatient treatment is available at the facility?

▶ Does this facility offer a full range of services for transition back into society (i.e., transitional living programs, driver's education, supported employment opportunities, social services, etc.)?

The doctor and hospital staff will be working with a case manager, who will assist in determining what sort of rehabilitation services a person may benefit from. The case manager acts in part as an advocate for the patient as he or she moves through the health care system. Case managers also serve as a liaison or contact with insurance companies and county and state aid programs, making sure a patient makes maximum use of benefits.

If the patient is referred to a rehabilitation provider that is a separate facility from the general hospital where he was treated, family members should take a tour of the facility as soon as possible. This can usually be arranged by either talking with the case manager or by calling the facilities patient services department.

Checking out the facility will give family members an opportunity to find out more about what their loved one can expect from his stay and his course of treatment. It also provides a chance to raise any concerns or questions they may have. The staff at the rehabilitation facility will probably be better prepared to answer questions about what a person can expect at their facility than the doctor at the general hospital who is making the referral.

Resources

As stated in the introduction to this book, knowledge is indeed power when it comes to navigating America's health care system. While you or your family may at first feel lost on such a journey, there are associations, support groups, institutions, hotlines, and other great sources that you can tap into for help. The trick is knowing where to look and how to find them. Of course, your doctor is always a good place to start, and the social workers at your local hospital are walking encyclopedias who are experts at referrals. Remember, it doesn't cost anything to call and ask them for help, and you can do so anonymously, if that's a concern.

The importance of the internet and the world wide web cannot be understated. Both are excellent sources of information for people in search of the best health care possible. Nearly every major hospital, medical center, research facility and health care association has a web site. Medical experts, caregiver support groups and patient advocates all use internet newsgroups to share information. What would take you a week to track down at 10 different libraries can be accessed in a matter of a few hours on the web or internet.

A young mother recently told me about the day her son was diagnosed with a mild form of autism. Even though she had spent months talking with a stream of doctors and specialists, she recalled how lost and alone she felt when the diagnosis was finally made. This despite the talk the doctor gave her and some of the pamphlets with which she was sent home. That night, she poured herself a cup of coffee and sat down at the computer, where she started what would be a two week cyber-based crash course in autism, tracking down literally every source around the world that was available on the subject—and all without leaving her upstairs den.

She supplemented this knowledge and shaped it to her specific case by remaining in close contact with her primary care physician. The more she learned about autism, the more she was able to cope with her fears about her son's future. During subsequent visits to her son's doctor, she was more inclined to ask him questions and felt as if she understood more of what he told her.

Her experience is a good example of how health care consumers can use the internet and web to their advantage. The mass of information at your disposal can be daunting, such as when you type in "Cancer" for your web search and come back with 250,000 sites. Still, with a bit of practice you can learn how to focus your search more accurately, enabling you to jump on the fast lane of the "Information Super Highway." If you don't have internet access at home, try the library or a local university—both are likely to have computer labs and technicians who can help you with your search.

Presented here is a list of resources categorized by illness or disability and/or the community they serve. Where possible, phone numbers, 800 numbers, TDDs, fax numbers, e-mail addresses and web site addresses have been included along with the standard mailing address. It is also noted if the group or association publishes material or offers educational videotapes.

And remember, this list is just a start—literally only a fraction of what's out there. If you contact a resource from this list, ask them for additional sources.

AIDS

AIDS/HIV Nightline
P.O. Box 191350
San Francisco, California
94119-1350
1-800-273-AIDS

AIDS National Interface
Network
110 Maryland Avenue NE
Suite 504
Washington D.C. 20002
(202) 842-0010

American Red Cross Office of
HIV/AIDS Education
431 18th Street NW
Washington, D.C. 20006
(202) 726-6693

HIV Viral Load Testing
1-888-HIV-LOAD
(This toll-free number provides a national directory of centers that offer free testing for your HIV viral load.)

National HIV/AIDS
Hotline
1-800-342-2437

National Organizations
Responding to AIDS
1828 L. Street NW Suite 802
Washington, D.C. 20036
(202) 986-1300

People of Color Against
AIDS Network
1200 S. Jackson Street Suite 25
Seattle, Washington 98144
(206) 322-7061

SisterLove, Inc.
1432 Donnelly Avenue SW
Atlanta, Georgia 30310
(404) 753-7733
(This is a non-profit advocacy
group for women with
HIV/AIDS)

Alzheimer's

Alzheimer's Association
919 Michigan Avenue
Suite 1000
Chicago, Illinois 60611
(312) 335-8700
1-800-272-3900
(This association can provide
information on local
Alzheimer's Association chapters across the country.)

Alzheimer's Disease Education
and Research
PO Box 8250
Silver Springs, Maryland
20907-8250
1-800-438-4380

Blindness

AT&T Accessible Communi-
cations Products Center
5 Wood Hollow Road
Suite 1119
Parsippany, New Jersey 07054
1-800-233-1222 & TDD
(The company's resource for
the vision and hearing
impaired.)

Canine Companions for
Independence
4350 Occidental Road
PO Box 446
Santa Rosa, California
95402-0446
1-800-572-2275

Eye Bank Association of
America
1001 Connecticut Avenue NW
Suite 601
Washington, D.C. 20036-5504
(202) 775-4999

National Society to
Prevent Blindness
500 East Remington Road
Schaumberg, Illinois 60173
(847) 843-2020

Resources

Cancer

American Brain Tumor
Association
2720 River Road Suite 146
Des Plaines, Illinois
60018-4110
1-800-886-2282
(847) 827-9910
(847) 827-9918–fax
abta@aol.com–e-mail

American Cancer Society
1599 Clifton Road NE
Atlanta, Georgia 30329
1-800-ACS-2345
1-800-422-6237
mneitzel@mindspring.com–
e-mail

The Association for the Cure
of Cancer of the Prostate
(CaP CURE)
1250 Fourth Street Suite 360
Santa Monica, California
90401-1353
(310) 458-2873
(310) 458-8074–fax

Cancer Care Inc.
1130 Avenue of the Americas
New York, New York 10036
(212) 302-2400

Candlelighters Childhood
Cancer Foundation
7190 Woodmont Ave. Ste. 460

Bethesda, Maryland 20814
(301) 657-8401
1-800-366-2223

City of Hope National
Medical Center
1500 East Duarte Road
Duarte, California 91010-3000
(818) 359-8111

Leukemia Society of America
600 Third Avenue 4th Floor
New York, New York 10016
(212) 573-8484

National Alliance of Breast
Cancer Organizations
9 East 37th Street 10th Floor
New York, New York 10016
NABCOinfo@aol.com–e-mail

National Cancer Institutes
Office of Cancer Communications, Building 31-2B10
9000 Rockville Pike
Bethesda, Maryland 20892
1-800-422-6237

National Childhood
Cancer Foundation
440 E. Huntington Drive
Suite 300
PO Box 60012
Arcadia, California
91066-6012
1-800-458-6223
1-800-723-2822–fax

National Coalition for
Cancer Survivorship
1010 Wayne Avenue Suite 300
Silver Spring, Maryland 20910
(301) 650-8868

National Kidney Cancer
Association
1234 Sherman Avenue
Evanston, Illinois 60202
(847) 332-1051
(847) 328-4425–fax
(847) 332-1052–BBS

Cerebral Palsy

United Cerebral Palsy
Associations
1600 L Street, NW
Washington, D.C. 20036-5602
1-800-USA-5UCP
(202) 776-0406–TDD
(202) 776-0414–fax
ucpanatl@ucpa.org–e-mail

**Consumer Advocacy
Groups**

People's Medical Society
462 Walnut Street
Allentown, Pennsylvania
18102
(610) 770-1670

Public Citizen Health
Research Group
2000 P Street
Washington, D.C. 20036
(202) 588-1000

National Association of
Social Workers
180 N. Michigan Avenue
Suite 400
Chicago, Illinois 60601
(312) 236-8308
(312) 236-6627–fax

Society for Healthcare
Consumer Advocacy
American Hospital Association
840 North Lake Shore Drive
Chicago, Illinois 60611
(312) 422-3999

Drug Abuse

Al-Anon Family Group
Headquarters
Box 862
Midtown Station
New York, NY 10018-0862
(757) 563-1600
1-800-356-9996
1-800-344-2666

American Council on
Alcoholism
5024 Campbell Blvd. Suite H
Baltimore, Maryland 21236
1-800-527-5344

Cocaine Anonymous
3740 Overland Avenue Suite H
Los Angeles, California 90034
(310) 559-5833
1-800-347-8998

Families Anonymous
PO Box 3475
Culver City, California 90231
(310) 313-5800
1-800-736-9805
(Provides help to families and
loved ones of teens abusing
drugs.)

National Drug Information
Center
2296 Henderson Mill Road
Suite 300
Atlanta, Georgia 30345
(770) 934-6364

National Institute on Drug
Abuse Hotline
5600 Fishers Lane Suite 10-05
Rockville, Maryland 20857
1-800-662-4357
1-800-662-9832–Spanish

Government Agencies

Centers For Disease Control
and Prevention
1600 Clifton Road NE
Atlanta, Georgia 30333
(404) 639-3311
netinfo@cdc1.cdc.gov–e-mail

Food and Drug Administration
Department of Health and
Human Services
5600 Fishers Lane, Room 16-85
Rockville, Maryland 20857
(301) 827-4420

National Institute of Health
5333 Westbard Avenue
Bethesda, Maryland 20892
1-800-352-9424

Head Injury

National Head Injury
Foundation, Inc.
1776 Massachusetts Ave. NW
Suite 100
Washington, D.C. 20036
(202) 296-6443
1-800-444-6443

Hearing Impaired

American Hearing Research
Foundation
55 East Washington Street
Suite 2022
Chicago, Illinois 60602
(312) 726-9670

American Speech, Language &
Hearing Association
10801 Rockville Pike
Rockville, Maryland 20852
(301) 897-5700
(301) 897-0157–TDD
1-800-638-8255

Hearing Helpline
PO Box 1840
Washington D.C. 20013
(703) 642-0580–Voice & TDD
1-800-327-9355–Voice & TDD

Kidney Patients

American Association of
Kidney Patients
1 Davis Boulevard Suite LL1
Tampa, Florida 33606
(813) 223-7099

American Kidney Fund
8110 Executive Boulevard
Rockville, Maryland 20852
1-800-638-8299

National Kidney Foundation
30 East 33rd Street
New York, New York 10016
(212) 889-2210
1-800-622-9010

Liver Disease

American Association for the
Study of Liver Disease
6900 Grove Road
Thorofare, New Jersey 08086
(609) 848-1000

American Liver Foundation
1425 Pompton Avenue
Cedar Grove, New Jersey
07009
1-800-223-0179

Maternity

Healthy Mothers, Healthy
Babies Coalition
409-12th Street SW
Washington, D.C. 20024
(202) 863-2552
(202) 863-2458

La Leche League International
9616 Minneapolis Avenue
PO Box 1209
Franklin Park, Illinois
60131-8209
1-800-LA-LECHE
(This group promotes breast

National Center for Education
in Maternal and Child Health
38th and R Streets NW
Washington, D.C. 20057
(202) 625-8400
feeding.)

**Medical Associations,
Academies and Boards**

American Academy of
Cosmetic Surgery
401 N. Michigan Avenue
Chicago, Illinois 60611
(312) 527-6713

American Academy of
Family Physicians
8880 Ward Parkway
Kansas City, Missouri 64114
(816) 333-9700

American Academy of
Orthopedic Surgeons
6300 North River Road
Rosemont, Illinois 60018
1-800-824-BONE

American Academy of Physical
Medicine and Rehabilitation
122 South Michigan Avenue
Suite 300
Chicago, Illinois 60603
(312) 464-9700

American Association of
Immunologists
9650 Rockville Pike
Bethesda, Maryland 20814
(301) 530-7178

American Association of
Neurological Surgeons
22 South Washington Street
Park Ridge, Illinois 60068

American Board of
Emergency Medicine
200 Woodland Pass Suite D
East Lansing, Michigan 48823
(517) 332-4800

American Board of
Family Practice
2228 Young Drive
Lexington, Kentucky 40505
(606) 269-5626

American Board of
Medical Specialties
180 Allen Road South Building
Suite 330
Atlanta, Georgia 30328
1-800-776-2378

American Board of
Obstetrics and Gynecology
4225 Roosevelt Way NE
Suite 305
Seattle, Washington 98105
(206) 223-6191

American Board of
Orthopedic Surgery
737 North Michigan Avenue
Suite 1150
Chicago, Illinois 60611
(312) 644-6610

American Board of Surgery
1617 John F. Kennedy Blvd.
Suite 860
Philadelphia, PA 19103-1847
(215) 568-4000

American Healthcare
Association
1201 L Street NW
Washington D.C. 20005
(202) 842-4444

American Medical Association
515 North State Street
Chicago, Illinois 60610
(312) 464-5000

American Nurses Association
600 Maryland Avenue SW
Suite 100 West
Washington, D.C. 20024-2571
(202) 554-4444
1-800-274-4ANA

Multiple Sclerosis

National Multiple
Sclerosis Society
1-800-FIGHT-MS
1-800-344-4867
info@nmss.org–e-mail

NMSS California Chapters:

NMSS
Central California Chapter
334 Shaw Suite 121
Clovis, California 93612
(209) 325-9293
(209) 325-9295–fax

NMSS
Northern California Chapter
150 Grand Avenue
Oakland, California 94612
(510) 268-0572
(510) 451-8796–fax
can@nmss.org–e-mail

NMSS
Southern California Chapter
230 N. Maryland Ave. Ste. 303
Glendale, CA 91206-4261
(818) 247-1175
(818) 247-1364–fax
cal@nmss.org–e-mail

NMSS New York Chapters:

NMSS
Long Island Chapter
200 Parkway Drive South
Suite 101
Hauppauge, New York 11788
(516) 864-8337
(516) 864-8342–fax

NMSS
New York City Chapter
30 West 26th Street 9th Floor
New York, New York 10010-2094
(212) 463-7787
(212) 989-4362–fax

NMSS
Northeastern
New York Chapter
9 Columbia Circle
Albany, New York 12203
(518) 464-0630
(518) 464-1234–fax

NMSS
South Central
New York Chapter
32 West State Street 1st Floor
Binghamton, NY 13901
(607) 724-5464–Tel/fax

Resources

Pharmacy

American Pharmaceutical
Association
2215 Constitution Ave. NW
Washington D.C. 20037-2985
(202) 628-4410
(202) 783-2351–fax
1-800-237-2742

National Pharmaceutical
Council
1894 Preston White Drive
Reston, Virginia 22091
(703) 620-6390
(703) 476-0904–fax

Pulmonary

American Lung Association
1740 Broadway
New York, New York
10019-4374
(212) 315-8700
(212) 265-5642–fax

Cystic Fibrosis Foundation
6931 Arlington Road
Bethesda, Maryland 20814
(301) 951-4422
1-800-344-4823

Lung Line
1400 Jackson Street
Denver, Colorado 80206
(303) 355-5864
(303) 398-1848–fax
1-800-222-5864

Rehabilitation

American Rehabilitation
Association
1910 Association Drive
Suite 200
Reston, Virginia 22091
(703) 648-9300
1-800-368-3513

National Rehabilitation
Information Center
8455 Colesville Road Suite 935
Silver Spring, Maryland
20910-3319
(301) 588-9284
(301) 587-1967–fax
1-800-346-2742–Voice & TDD
1-800-227-0216–Voice & TDD

Spinal Cord Injuries & Paralysis

American Paralysis Association
500 Morris Avenue
Springfield, New Jersey 07081
(973) 379-2690

American Syringomyelia
Alliance Project, Inc.
P.O. Box 1586
Longview, Texas 75606-1586
(214) 759-2469
1-800-ASAP-282
(ASAP is a national, non-profit
organization founded as a support network for people with
syringomyelia, a rare spinal
cord disorder. The project
publishes newsletters, brochures and educational
articles.)

Casa Colina Centers
for Rehabilitation
2850 North Garey Avenue
PO Box 6001
Pomona, CA 91769-6001
(909) 596-7733
(909) 593-0153–fax
ccrehab@lightside.com–e-mail
www.medaccess.com/scenters/
casacolina/cchome.htm–
web page
(A non-profit rehabilitation
institution that publishes a
variety of educational material
and videos on spinal cord
injury, traumatic brain injury,
stroke, wound care and other
conditions.)

National Paralysis Foundation
14651 Dallas Parkway
Suite 136
Dallas, Texas 75248
(972) 248-7100

National SCI Association
600 West Cummings Park
Suite 2000
Woburn, Massachusetts 01801
1-800-962-9629

National Spinal Cord
Injury Association
545 Concord Avenue Suite 29
Cambridge, MA 02138
(301) 588-6959
(301) 528-6959–fax
(This association publishes
national and local resource
directories for people with
spinal cord injuries, as well as
informational booklets and
serial publications.)

Paralyzed Veterans of America
Communication Program
801 18th Street NW
Washington, D.C. 20006
(202) 872-1300
1-800-424-8200
(This group serves veterans as
well as others with disabilities.
The group publishes two magazines: *Paraplegia News* and
Sports 'n Spokes. They also dis-
tribute educational videos.)

Spina Bifida Association
of America
4590 MacArthur Boulevard
NW Suite 250
Washington, D.C. 20007-4226
(202) 944-3285
1-800-621-3141
(This association publishes a
variety of brochures and
reports for both children and
adults, as well as educational
videos.)

Spinal Cord Society
Rural Road 5
Fergus Falls, Minnesota 56537
(218) 739-5252
(SCS is an advocacy organization that is working to help
find a cure for spinal cord
injuries. It has a computerized
data and referral service.
It also publishes a monthly
newsletter.)

Stroke

National Institute of Neurological Disorders and Strokes
P.O. Box 5801
Bethesda, Maryland 20824
1-800-352-9424

National Rehabilitation Hospital Stroke Recovery Program
102 Irving Street N.W.
Washington, D.C. 20010-2921
(202) 877-4NRH

National Stroke Association
8480 E. Orchard Rd. Ste. 1000
Engelwood, Colorado
80111-5015
1-800-STROKES
(This association publishes
booklets and brochures for
stroke survivors, their family
members and caregivers. They
also publish a stroke recovery
guide. A list of titles is available
upon request.)

Stroke Connection/
American Heart Association
National Center
7272 Greenville Avenue
Dallas, Texas 75231-4596
1-800-553-6321
(A national network that links
stroke survivors, their families
and health care professionals.
This association can provide
local support referrals through
their toll-free line. The association also publishes a newsletter six times a year, much of it
written by stroke survivors.)

Urological

Bladder Health Council
300 W. Pratt Suite 401
Baltimore, Maryland 21201
1-800-242-2383

Miscellaneous

Center for Accessible Housing
North Carolina
State University
PO Box 8613
Raleigh, North Carolina
27695-8613
1-800-647-6777

Center for Independent Living
2539 Telegraph Avenue
Berkeley, California 94704
(510) 841-4776

National Women's
Health Network
1325 G Street NW
Lower Level
Washington D.C. 20005
(202) 347-1140

**Publications, Books,
Catalogs & Directories**

Directory of Head Injury
Rehabilitation Services
1776 Massachusetts Avenue
NW Suite 100
Washington, D.C. 20036
(202) 296-6443
(A directory of services for
people with traumatic brain
injuries published by the
National Head Injury
Foundation Inc.)

The Hospital Phone Book
121 Chanlon Road
New Providence, New Jersey
07974
1-800-521-8110
(908) 665-3560–fax
(A comprehensive guide to
hospitals in the United States,
as well as a resource directory,
published by the U.S. Directory Service. Cost: $109.95)

New Mobility
23815 Stuart Ranch Road
Malibu, California 90265
(310) 317-4522
(310) 317-9644–fax
(A cutting edge lifestyle magazine for wheelchair-users
published by Miramar Com-
munications. The company
also publishes *HomeCare
Magazine* and several other
publications.

Research Medical
1603 Monrovia Avenue
Costa Mesa, California 92627
1-800-228-3643
(714) 548-9980
(714) 548-9967–fax
(A medical supply firm that
carries everything from urological and skin care products
to mobility and bathroom aids.
They also publish a detailed
catalog.)

Spinal Network–
The Total Wheelchair Book
PO Box 8987
Malibu, California 90265
1-800-543-4116
(310) 317-9644–fax
(A nearly 600-page resource
guide for wheelchair users
published by Miramar
Communications.)

Sports 'n Spokes
2111 East Highland Avenue
Suite 180
Phoenix, Arizona 85016-4702
(602) 224-0500
(602) 224-0507–fax
snsmagaz@aol.com–e-mail
(A bi-monthly sporting publi-
cation for wheelchair users.)

The Patient's Bill of Rights

In 1973, the American Hospital Association drafted a Patient's Bill of Rights. It has been adopted by most hospitals, many of which have either added to it or amended it for their institution. You should ask your local hospital for a copy of their Patient's Bill of Rights.

The Patient's Bill of Rights

I. The patient has the right to considerate and respectful care.

II. The patient has the right and is encouraged to obtain from physicians and other direct caregivers relevant, current and understandable information concerning diagnosis, treatment and prognosis.

Except in emergencies when the patient lacks decision-making capacity and the need for treatment is urgent, the patient is entitled to the opportunity to discuss and request information related to the specific procedures and/or treatments, the risks involved, the possible length of recuperation and the medically reasonable alternatives and their accompanying risks and benefits.

Patients have the right to know the identity of physicians, nurses and others involved in their care, as well as when those involved are students, residents and other trainees.

The patient also has the right to know the immediate and long-term financial implications of treatment choices, insofar as they are known.

III. The patient has the right to make decisions about the plan of care prior to and during the course of treatment and to refuse a recommended treatment or plan of care to the extent permitted by law and hospital policy and to be informed of the medical consequences of his action.

In case of such refusal, the patient is entitled to other appropriate care and services that the hospital provides or transfer to another hospital. The hospital should notify patients of any policy that might affect patient choice within the institution.

IV. The patient has the right to have an advance directive (such as a living will, health care proxy or durable power of attorney for health care) concerning treatment or designating a surrogate decision maker with the expectation that the hospital will honor the intent of that directive to the extent permitted by law and hospital policy.

Health care institutions must advise patients of their rights under state law and hospital policy to make informed medical choices, ask if the patients has an advance directive and include that information in patient records. The patient has the right to timely information about hospital policy that may limit its ability to implement fully a legal valid advance directive.

V. The patient has the right to every consideration of privacy. Case discussion, consultation, examination and treatment should be conducted so as to protect each patient's privacy.

VI. The patient has the right to expect that all communications and records pertaining to his/her care will be treated as confidential by the hospital, except in such cases as suspected abuse and public health hazards when reporting is permitted or required by law. The patient has the right to expect that the hospital will emphasize the confidentiality of this information when it releases it to any other parties entitled to review information in these records.

VII. The patient has the right to review the records pertaining to his/her medical care and to have the information explained or interpreted as necessary, except when restricted by law.

VIII. The patient has the right to expect that, within its capacity and policies, a hospital will make reasonable response to the request of a patient for appropriate and medically indicated care and services. The hospital must provide evaluation, service and/or referral as indicated by the urgency of the case. When medically appropriate and legally permissible, or when a patient has so requested, a patient may be transferred to another facility. The institution which the patient is to be transferred must first have accepted the patient for transfer. The patient must also have the benefit of complete information and explanation concerning the need for, risks, benefits and alternatives to such a transfer.

IX. The patient has the right to ask and be informed of the existence of business relationships among the hospital, educational institutions, other health care providers or payers that may influence the patient's treatment and care.

X. The patient has the right to consent to or decline to participate in proposed research studies or human experimentation affecting care and treatment or requiring direct patient involvement and to have those studies fully explained prior to consent. A patient who declines to participate in research or experimentation is entitled to the most effective care that the hospital can otherwise provide.

XI. The patient has the right to expect reasonable continuity of care when appropriate and to be informed by physicians and other caregivers of available and realistic patient care options when hospital care is no longer appropriate.

XII. The patient has the right to be informed of hospital policies and practices that relate to patient care, treatment and responsibilities. The patient has the right to be informed of available resources for resolving disputes, grievances and conflicts, such as ethics committees, patient representatives , or other mechanisms available in the institution. The patient has the right to be informed of the hospital's charges for services and available payment methods.

Patient Rights, Part II

The American Hospital Association issued its Patient's Bill of Rights to provide a framework for hospitals around the nation to build upon. Most hospitals have done just that, using the basic concepts endorsed by the AHA, but customizing it with their own individual language. Often a hospital will include a patient right that was not first laid out in AHA's original manifesto.

To show you an example of just how a hospital will do this, the following is a list of patient rights that you might find in a typical American hospital:

I. You have the right to treatment regardless of race, creed, sex, national origin or sources of payment for care.

II. You have the right to be treated with respect and concern.

III. You have the right to: 1) know about your health and nature of any illness that you have; 2) have access to an interpreter if you do not understand the predominant language being spoken; 3) know the names, titles and job descriptions of those giving you health care and the name of your primary physician along with professional relationships of other physicians and non-physicians who will see you.

IV. You have the right to be given the best care available and to privacy and respect about your illness and care of that illness. Your doctor may have to talk to other hospital staff. This will be done in strict confidence and with your confidentiality protected.

V. You have the right to expect that all medical records and all other information about your care will be kept confidential. Your record may be read only by those directly involved in your care, by persons monitoring the quality of your care or by persons authorized by law or regulation. Any others must have your consent.

VI. You have the right to receive information about your health in order to give informed consent prior to the start of any procedure and/or treatment. When medically significant alternatives or care exist, you have the right to this information, prior to giving consent.

VII. You have the right to actively participate in decisions regarding your medical care. You also have the right to refuse treatment as permitted by law. If you refuse, you must be informed of the health risks associated with refusal of treatment. You have the right to participate in the consideration of ethical issues that arise in providing your care through the hospital's Ethics Committee.

VIII. You have the right to be transferred to another hospital if: 1) the treatment is for medical reasons; 2) your permission is obtained before you are sent to another hospital; 3) you are informed about the type of health care to be given at another hospital before giving permission before transfer; 4) your doctor or health care persons provide for continuity of your care.

IX. You have the right to consult with a specialist at your own request and expense.

X. You have the right to expect reasonable safety regarding hospital practices and the hospital environment.

XI. You have the right to obtain complete and current information regarding the diagnosis (evaluation), treatment and any known prognosis (recovery expectations) about your health. If it is not medically advisable to give you the information, it will be made available to your legally authorized representative.

XII. You have the right to request and receive an itemized and detailed explanation of the total bill for services rendered in the hospital.

XIII. You have the right to be informed of the hospital's rules and regulations applicable to your conduct as a patient. You have the right to voice complaints regarding the care received without fear of reprisal.

XIV. You have the right to be informed if the hospital proposes to engage in or perform any experimental or research /educational projects affecting your care or treatment , and you have the right to refuse to participate in any such activity.

XV. You have the right to designate a representative decision-maker in the event you become unable to communicate your wishes regarding care. You have the right to formulate an advance directive which makes your wishes known to all caregivers about life-sustaining and resuscitative care. This hospital agrees to comply with your wishes within all applicable legal limitations.

Patient Responsibilities

While the American Hospital Association has established the Patient's Bill of Rights, a health care manifesto that has been adapted by most hospitals in the nation (often with their own touch, as seen in Appendix B), hospitals also establish the responsibilities of the *patient*. These are usually contained, along with the Patient's Bill of Rights, in the literature (or patient guidebook) a hospital will provide a patient once she is admitted. If you can't find such a document in the admissions literature at your hospital, ask the supervising nurse if the hospital has such a document. If the hospital has a patient relations department, contact them for the information.

The following is an example of a hospital's patient's responsibilities document, this one drafted by Pomona Valley Hospital Medical Center.

I. You have the responsibility, along with those in the health profession, for seeing that your "Patient Rights" are followed.

II. You have the responsibility to provide all information (including prior treatment and other services) relating to your illness.

III. You have the responsibility, along with your physician, in planning for your complete care.

IV. You have the responsibility to follow your physician's instructions (including taking medicine ordered) after you have agreed to a treatment.

V. You have the responsibility to inform your physician if you cannot follow his or her recommendations.

VI. You are responsible for assuring that the financial obligations of your health care are fulfilled as promptly as possible.

VII. You have the responsibility to express your concerns or feeling regarding your treatment with the hospital staff.

VIII. You have the responsibility to follow hospital rules and regulations affecting patient care and conduct.

IX. You have the responsibility to be considerate of the rights and property of other patients and hospital associates, and to assist in the control of noise, smoking, and the number of visitors.

X. You are responsible for notifying the hospital staff or your physician if you do not understand the treatment being given or what is expected of you.

XI. You have the responsibility for keeping your appointments.

XII. You have the responsibility to assume the burden of your health care if you refuse treatment or do not follow the physician's or hospital staff's instructions.

XIII. You have the responsibility to provide a copy of your advance directive to the hospital so that it can be kept with your records.

Top 100 Hospitals
in the U.S.

Hospitals in the United States are ranked annually by the group HCIA-Mercer, which publishes a Top 100 list every year. What follows is the Top 100 hospitals as ranked in their most recent survey. Hospitals are listed in alphabetical order by state. They are broken down by their bed size, location (urban vs. rural) and whether or not it is teaching hospital. Not all states are represented because not every state had hospitals listed in the Top 100.

Legend for code:

　　U—Urban hospital with fewer than 250 beds.

　　R—Rural hospital with fewer than 250 beds.

　　N—Non-teaching hospital with 250 or more beds.

　　T—Teaching hospital with 250 or more beds.

　　M—Major teaching hospital with 400 or more beds.

Alabama

University of Alabama Hospital, Birmingham (M)

Arizona

Community Hospital, Wickenberg (U)
Mesa Lutheran Hospital, Mesa (N)
Mt. Graham Community Hospital, Safford (R)

California

Community Hospital of Huntington Park, Huntington
    Park (U)
Fountain Valley Regional Hospital & Medical Center,
    Fountain Valley (N)
Hospital of Barstow Inc., Barstow (U)
Lancaster Community Hospital, Lancaster (U)
Pomona Valley Hospital Medical Center, Pomona (N)
Queen of Angels/Hollywood Presbyterian Medical Center,
    Los Angeles (T)
St. Agnes Medical Center, Fresno (N)
The Medical Center at UCSF, San Francisco (M)
Tri–City Medical Center, Oceanside (T)

Colorado

Lutheran Medical Center, Wheat Ridge (N)
University Hospital, Denver (T)

Connecticut

Hartford Hospital, Hartford (M)

Florida

Baptist Medical Center, Jacksonville (T)
Columbia Aventura Hospital & Medical Center,
    Aventura (N)
Columbia Brandon Regional Medical Center, Brandon (N)

Columbia Gulf Coast Hospital, Fort Myers (U)
Columbia Kendall Regional Medical Center, Miami (N)
Columbia New Port Richey Hospital, New Port Richey (N)
Columbia Northwest Medical Center, Margate (U)
Columbia Orange Park Medical Center, Orange Park (U)
Columbia Regional Medical Center of Southwest Florida, Fort Myers (N)
Columbia University Hospital and Medical Center, Tamarac (U)
Leesburg Regional Medical Center, Leesburg (N)
Orlando Regional Medical Center, Orlando (T)
St. Vincent's Medical Center, Jacksonville (T)

Georgia

Candler Hospital, Savannah (N)
Flint River Community Hospital, Montezuma (R)
Hamilton Medical Center, Dalton (N)
Tanner Medical Center–Villa Rica, Villa Rica (U)

Illinois

Crossroads Community Hospital, Mount Vernon (R)
Evanston Hospital Corporation, Evanston (M)
Lutheran General Hospital, Park Ridge (M)
MacNeal Hospital, Berwyn (T)

Indiana

Deaconess Hospital, Evansville (T)
Parkview Memorial Hospital, Fort Wayne (T)
St. Mary's Medical Center–Evansville, Evansville (T)
Westview Hospital, Indianapolis (U)

Kansas

Goodland Regional Medical Center, Goodland (R)
St. Francis Hospital & Medical Center, Topeka (T)

Kentucky

Breckinridge Memorial Hospital, Hardinsburg (R)
Wayne County Hospital, Monticello (R)

Louisiana

West Jefferson Medical Center, Marrero (N)

Maryland

Mercy Medical Center, Baltimore (T)

Massachusetts

Beth Israel Deaconess Medical Center, Boston (M)
Brigham & Women's Hospital, Boston (M)
Columbia Metrowest Medical Center, Framingham (T)
St. Luke's Hospital of New Bedford, New Bedford (N)

Michigan

Blodgett Memorial Medical Center, Grand Rapids (T)
Providence Hospital & Medical Centers, Southfield (M)
St. Joseph Mercy Hospital, Ann Arbor (M)
W.A. Foote Memorial Hospital Inc., Jackson (N)

Minnesota

Buffalo Hospital, Buffalo (U)
Rochester Methodist Hospital, Rochester (T)

Missouri

Cox Health Systems, Springfield (T)
St. Luke's Hospital, Chesterfield (T)

New York

Staten Island University Hospital, Staten Island (M)
University Hospital & Medical Center at Stony Brook,
    Stony Brook (M)

North Carolina

Columbia Heritage Hospital, Tarboro (U)
Franklin Regional Medical Center, Louisburg (U)

North Dakota

Union Hospital, Mayville (R)

Ohio

Akron General Medical Center, Akron (M)
Cleveland Clinic Foundation, Cleveland (M)
Grant/Riverside Methodist Hospitals, Columbus (T)
Knox Community Hospital, Mount Vernon (R)
Mercy Medical Center, Springfield (N)
Meridia Hillcrest Hospital, Mayfield Heights (T)
St. Rita's Medical Center, Lima (N)

Oklahoma

Medical Center of Southeastern Oklahoma, Durant (R)

Oregon

Columbia Willamette Valley Medical Center,
McMinnville (U)

South Carolina

Medical University of South Carolina Medical Center,
Charleston (M)

South Dakota

Lookout Memorial Hospital, Spearfish (R)

Tennessee

Baptist Dekalb Hospital, Smithville (R)
Columbia Hendersonville Hospital, Hendorsonville (U)
Fentress County General Hospital, Jamestown (R)

Frank T. Rutherford Memorial Hospital Inc., Carthage (R)
Woods Memorial Hospital District, Etowah (R)

Texas

Brackenridge Hospital, Austin (T)
Columbia Clear Lake Regional Medical Center,
    Webster (N)
Harris Methodist Hospital–Fort Worth, Fort Worth (T)
Hermann Hospital, Houston (M)
Lake Pointe Medical Center, Rowlett (U)
Memorial Healthcare System, Houston (T)
Parkview Regional Hospital, Mexia (R)
Presbyterian Hospital of Dallas, Dallas (T)
R.E. Thomason General Hospital, El Paso (T)
Wood County Central Hospital, Quitman (R)

Utah

Alta View Hospital, Sandy (U)
Columbia Brigham City Community Hospital,
    Brigham City (R)
Columbia Castleview Hospital, Price (R)
Columbia Lakeview Hospital, Bountiful (U)

Virginia

Lee County Community Hospital, Pennington Gap (R)

Washington

Harrison Memorial Hospital, Bremerton (N)
St. Joseph Medical Center, Tacoma (T)

Wisconsin

Baldwin Hospital, Baldwin (U)
New London Family Medical Center, New London (U)
Waupun Memorial Hospital, Waupun (R)

State Insurance Regulators

Health care insurance is regulated by the states. Here are the government agencies in each state that regulate health plans. These agencies can provide consumers with important basic information about health insurance companies doing business in your state.

Director of Insurance
PO Box 110805
333 Willoughby Ave. 9th Floor
Juneau, Alaska 99811
(907) 465-2515

Insurance Commissioner
135 South Union Street
Montgomery, Alabama 36130
(334) 269-3550

Insurance Commissioner
University Tower Building
Suite 400
1123 South University Avenue
Little Rock, Arkansas 72204
(501) 686-2900

Director of Insurance
2910 North 44th St. Suite 210
Phoenix, Arizona 85018
(602) 912-8400

Commisioner of Corporations
Department of Corporations
3700 Wilshire Boulevard
Suite 600
Los Angeles, California 90010
(213) 736-3481

Insurance Commissioner
One City Centre Building
Suite 1120
770 L Street
Sacramento, California 95814
(916) 492-3500

Commissioner of Insurance
1560 Broadway Suite 850
Denver, Colorado 80202
(303) 894-7499

Insurance Commissioner
PO Box 816
Hartford, Connecticut 06142
(860) 297-3800

Insurance Commissioner
Rodney Building
841 Silver Lake Boulevard
Dover, Delaware 19901
(302) 739-4251

Insurance Commissioner
State Capital
Plaza Level 11
Tallahassee, Florida 32399
(904) 922-3100

Insurance Commissioner
2 Martin Luther King, Jr. Drive
Floyd Memorial Building
704 West Tower
Atlanta, Georgia 30334
(404) 656-2056

Insurance Commissioner
250 South King St. 5th Floor
Honolulu, Hawaii 96813
(808) 586-2790

Insurance Commissioner
Lucas State Office Building
6th Floor
Des Moines, Iowa 50319
(515) 281-5705

Insurance Director
700 West State St. 3rd Floor
Boise, Idaho 83720
(208) 334-2250

Insurance Director
320 West Washington Street
4th Floor
Springfield, Illinois 62767
(217) 782-4515

Insurance Commissioner
311 West Washington Street
Suite 300
Indianapolis, Indiana 46204
(317) 232-2385

Insurance Commissioner
420 S.W. 9th Street
Topeka, Kansas 66612
(913) 296-7801

Insurance Commissioner
215 West Main Street
Frankfort, Kentucky 40601
(502) 564-3630

Insurance Commissioner
470 Atlantic Avenue 6th Floor
Boston, Massachusettes 02210
(617) 521-7301

Insurance Commissioner
Stanbalt Building
7th Floor South
501 St. Paul Place
Baltimore, Maryland 21202
(410) 333-2521

Insurance Superintendent
State Office Building
State House Station No. 34
Augusta, Maine 04333
(207) 624-8475

Insurance Commissioner
611 West Ottawa Street
2nd Floor North
Lansing, Michigan 48933
(517) 373-9273

Insurance Commissioner
133 East 7th Street
St. Paul, Minneapolis 55101
(612) 296-6848

Insurance Commissioner
1804 Walter Sillers Building
Jackson, Mississippi 39205
(601) 354-7300

Insurance Director
301 West High St. Room 630
Jefferson City, Missouri 65101
(573) 751-4126

Insurance Commissioner
Mitchell Building Room 270
126 North Sanders
Helena, Montana 59620
(406) 444-2040

Insurance Director
Terminal Building Suite 400
941 O Street
Lincoln, Nebraska 68508
(402) 471-2201

Insurance Commissioner
Dobbs Building Suite 3067
Raleigh, North Carolina 27603
(919) 733-7349

Insurance Commissioner
600 East Boulevard
Bismark, North Dakota 58505
(701) 328-2440

Insurance Commissioner
169 Manchester Street
Concord, New Hampshire
03301
(603) 271-2261

Insurance Commissioner
20 West State Street
CN 325
Trenton, New Jersey 08625
(609) 292-5363

Insurance Superintendent
P.O. Box 1269
Santa Fe, New Mexico 87504
(505) 827-4500

Insurance Superintendent
160 West Broadway
New York, New York 10013
(212) 602-0420

Insurance Commissioner
1665 Hot Springs Road
Carson City, Nevada 89716
(702) 687-4270

Insurance Director
2100 Stella Court
Columbus, Ohio 43215
(614) 644-2658

Insurance Commissioner
1901 North Walnut
Oklahoma City, Oklahoma
73152
(405) 521-2828

Insurance Commissioner
21 Labor & Industries Building
Salem, Oregon 97310
(503) 947-7980

Insurance Commissioner
Strawberry Square 13th Floor
Harrisburg, Pennsylvania 17120
(717) 787-5193 or
(717) 787-2317

Insurance Commissioner
233 Richmond Street Suite 233
Providence, Rhode Island 02903
(401) 277-2223

Insurance Commissioner
1612 Marion Street
Columbia, South Carolina 29202
(803) 737-6160

Insurance Director
500 E. Capitol
Pierre, South Dakota 57501
(605) 773-3563

Insurance Commissioner
Volunteer Plaza
5000 James Roberston Parkway
Nashville, Tennessee 37243
(615) 741-2241

Insurance Commissioner
PO Box 149104
333 Guadalupe Street
Austin, Texas 78714
(512) 463-6464

Insurance Commissioner
3110 State Office Building
Room 3110
Salt Lake City, Utah 84114
(801) 538-3800

Insurance Commissioner
89 Main Street Drawer 20
Montpelier, Vermont 05620
(802) 828-3301

Insurance Commissioner
1300 East Main Street
Richmond, Virginia 23219
(804) 371-9694

Insurance Commissioner
Insurance Building
PO Box 40255
Olympia, Washington 98504
(206) 753-7300

Insurance Commissioner
441 4th Street NW
8th Floor North
Washington, D.C. 20001
(202) 727-7426

Insurance Commissioner
PO Box 50540
2019 E. Washington Street
Charleston, West Virginia
25305
(304) 558-3394

Insurance Commissioner
121 East Wilson
Madison, Wisconsin 53703
(608) 266-0102

Insurance Commissioner
Herschler Building
122 West 25th Street
Cheyenne, Wyoming 82002
(307) 777-7401

Glossary of Terms

Acute: A condition that is marked by symptoms that are severe, develop quickly and don't last for a long time.

Alternative Medicine: Sometimes called "complimentary medicine," this term is used to describe treatments and therapies—often practiced by other cultures for thousands of years—that fall outside of traditional Western medicine.

Angiogram: An X-ray of a blood vessel.

Ambulatory Care: Treatment that is administered on an outpatient basis, meaning that it does not involve admission to a hospital. Usually provided in a clinic, doctor's office or community health center.

Anniversary Date: The date on which your health plan is renewed every year, usually preceded by an "open enrollment period" during which you have the opportunity to switch plans.

Benefits: The health care services that will be provided to you through your insurance company, such as hospitalization, outpatient treatments, pharmaceutical drugs, etc.

Bypass: Surgery in which a vein is removed from another part of the patient's body and grafted into the heart, between the aorta and a coronary artery, bypassing a dangerous blockage.

Caesarean Section: A birth delivery through an incision made in the stomach and uterus.

Capitation: A method in which HMOs pay service providers (doctors and hospitals) a set fee every month no matter how many patients from that health plan they treat.

Cardiologist: A heart doctor.

Case Manager: The person who coordinates your health care, working with you, your hospital's staff, your doctor, and your insurance company. This person is basically a liaison who ensures your care is coordinated among all the parties involved. Case managers often are employees of insurance companies.

Chronic Obstructive Pulmonary Disease (COPD): A collection of chronic lung disorders, such as emphysema and asthma, which are often referred to under the umbrella term "lung disease."

Chemotherapy: A cancer treatment that involves the intravenous administration of toxic chemicals that kill the malignant cells.

Claim: The document that is submitted to an insurance company by the health care provider which reports the treatment given. A claim is essentially a payment invoice.

Clinician: A health care worker who works out of a clinic. This broad term is generally used to cover a range of professionals, including doctors, nurses and therapists.

Computerized Axial Tomography (CAT Scan): A radiological technique that produces internal views of the body in the form of thin slices.

Co-payment: The cost you will have to pay under your health plan when receiving medical treatment, sometimes called an "out-of-pocket" expense. Co-payments are often just fractions of the total cost, such as a $5 co-payment on a $45 doctor's office visit.

Deductible: Another out-of-pocket expense, often associated with traditional indemnity insurance plans. A deductible is the amount you pay for medical care before your insurance kicks in. For example, if you have a $1000 deductible and have paid $900 in medical fees over the course of the year, you have $100 left before you meet your deductible and your insurance company begins to pay for your medical expenses.

Dermatologist: A doctor who specializes in the treatment of skin disorders.

Echocardiogram: Technology which bounces ultrasound waves off of the heart in order to detect deformities or problems with heart valves.

Electrocardiogram (EKG): A record of heart muscle activity, gathered by electrodes placed on the chest, which can detect heart damage. Used to determine whether a person has suffered a heart attack.

Electroencephalogram (EEG): A record of brain patterns, gathered by electrodes placed on the skull, which can detect brain damage.

Enrollment Area: The geographic area in which you must live in order to be covered by certain health plans.

Fee-for-Service: The traditional style of health insurance in which doctors and hospitals bill insurance companies for services rendered.

Gatekeeper: The primary care doctor in an HMO who will coordinate and authorize your care throughout the organization's system.

Gynecologist: A specialist in the female reproductive system.

Health Screening: The battery of tests insurance companies use to determine if you have "preexisting" conditions or are at risk for other diseases.

Inpatient: A type of hospital care or treatment which requires at least one overnight stay.

Internist: A doctor who specializes in the diagnosis and non-surgical treatment of diseases.

Labor, Delivery, Recovery, Postpartum (LDRPs): The new style of rooms hospitals use for women giving birth, it combines all of the necessary functions for each stage of the birthing process, thus preventing the mother from getting shuffled to a variety of different rooms.

Licensed Practical Nurse (LPN): LPNs have a lower level of training than a registered nurse. However, LPNs have many of the same responsibilities as RNs.

Nephrologist: A doctor who specializes in kidney disorders.

Network: The health care providers—hospitals, physician groups, doctors and clinics—who are contracted to deliver services for a health plan.

Nurses Aide: An assistant to RNs and LPNs who may check your blood pressure and other vital signs, but may not administer shots or give medicine.

Obstetrician: A doctor who specializes in pregnancy and childbirth.

Occupational Therapy (OT): The treatment therapy that helps a patient rebuild "life skills" (such as balance, coordination and body control) that may have been lost due to an accident or illness.

Ophthalmologist: A doctor who specializes in eye problems.

Orthopedist: A doctor who specializes in bone problems.

Otorhinolaryngologist (ENT): An ear, nose and throat specialist.

Pediatrician: A doctor who specializes in the medical care of children.

Physiatrist: A doctor who specializes in physical disabilities, such as amputees.

Physical Therapy (PT): The treatment therapy that uses exercises, hydrotherapy and other procedures to strengthen muscles, joints and other body parts weakened by illness or injury.

Physician Assistant: A health care professional who can legally assume many of the duties of a physician.

Preexisting Condition: A medical condition that a person developed before he applied for health coverage.

Primary Care Physician: The doctor who is the starting point for your health care. He will deliver most treatments in his office, will recommend specialists when necessary, and will coordinate any additional medical care as needed.

Radiation: A treatment for cancer that involves targeting select areas, such as malignant tumors, with doses of radiation in order to destroy the cancerous cells.

Radiologist: A specialist who uses radioactive substances (especially X-rays) in the diagnosis and treatment of a variety of diseases.

Referral: When one doctor recommends that you receive treatment from another physician. This usually occurs when your primary care doctor feels a specialist's advice or service is needed to diagnose or treat your illness.

Registered Nurse (RN): The most experienced type of nurse, specially trained and state-licensed. They can administer shots and give medicine.

Ultrasound: Ultrasonic radiation used to image organs in the body. It is often used to get a picture of a fetus in the mother's womb.

Urologist: A doctor who specializes in the urinary tract and prostate gland.

Vital Signs: The basic signs of life, including your temperature, pulse (heartbeat) and respiration (breathing) rate.

Workup: The battery of tests and examinations used to make a diagnosis.

Heath Care Handbook
A Consumer's Guide to the
American Health Care System
by Mark Cromer
256 pages $12.95

The Book of Good Habits
Simple and Creative Ways to
Enrich Your Life
by Dirk Mathison
224 pages $9.95

Offbeat Museums
The Curators and Collections
of America's Most Unusual
Museums
by Saul Rubin
232 pages $17.95

Helpful Household Hints
by June King
224 pages $12.95

How to Win Lotteries,
Sweepstakes, and Contests
by Steve Ledoux
224 pages $12.95

Letter Writing Made Easy!
Featuring Sample Letters for
Hundreds of Common Occasions
by Margaret McCarthy
224 pages $12.95

How to Find Your
Family Roots
The Complete Guide to Searching
for Your Ancestors
by William Latham
224 pages $12.95

1-800-784-9553

Health Care Handbook   _____

The Book of Good Habits   _____

Offbeat Museums   _____

Helpful Household Hints   _____

How to Win Lotteries, Sweepstakes, and Contests   _____

Letter Writing Made Easy!   _____

How to Find Your Family Roots   _____

Subtotal   _____

Shipping and Handling (see below)   _____

CA residents add 8.25% sales tax   _____

Total   _____

Name _____

Address _____

City _____ State _____ Zip _____

Card Number _____ Exp _____

☐ Visa   ☐ MasterCard

Signature _____

☐ Enclosed is my check or money order payable to:

Santa Monica Press	**Shipping and Handling**
P.O. Box 1076	1 book $3.00
Dept. 4670	2–3 books $4.00
Santa Monica, CA 90406	Each additional book is $ .50

1-800-784-9553

DATE DUE

NOV 1 0 1999		
JUN 0 1 2002		
JUL 2 8 2005		
GAYLORD		PRINTED IN U.S.A.